The Growth and Influence of Islam
IN THE NATIONS OF ASIA AND CENTRAL ASIA

Islamism and Terrorist Groups in Asia

The Growth and Influence of Islam

IN THE NATIONS OF ASIA AND CENTRAL ASIA

Afghanistan

Azerbaijan

Bangladesh

Indonesia

Islam in Asia: Facts and Figures

Islamism and Terrorist Groups in Asia

Kazakhstan

The Kurds

Kyrgyzstan

Malaysia

Muslims in China

Muslims in India

Muslims in Russia

Pakistan

Tajikistan

Turkmenistan

Uzbekistan

The Growth and Influence of Islam

IN THE NATIONS OF ASIA AND CENTRAL ASIA

Islamism and Terrorist Groups in Asia

Michael Radu

Mason Crest Publishers
Philadelphia

Produced by OTTN Publishing, Stockton, New Jersey

Mason Crest Publishers
370 Reed Road
Broomall, PA 19008
www.masoncrest.com

First printing

1 3 5 7 9 8 6 4 2

Library of Congress Cataloging-in-Publication Data

Radu, Michael.
 Islamism and terrorist groups in Asia / Michael Radu.
    p. cm. — (Growth and influence of Islam in the nations of Asia and Central Asia)
 Includes bibliographical references and index.
 ISBN 1-59084-834-9
 1. Islam and politics. 2. Islam and politics—Asia. 3. Terrorism—Religious aspects—
Islam. I. Title. II. Series.
 BP173.7.R29 2005
 303.6'25'088297095—dc22

                              2005002755

Author's Acknowledgments

Nothing in this text would have been possible without the cooperation of the
Foreign Policy Research Institute, my employer for two decades, and, especially,
without the contribution of Ms. Trudy Kuehner. I thank them all, and reserve the
merits and blame for this text for myself.

Table of Contents

Protesters burn an American flag during a demonstration in Karachi, Pakistan. Anger at U.S. policies—which some Muslims contend are anti-Islamic—is believed to be one factor in the rise of militant Islamism and terrorism in Asia.

Dr. Harvey Sicherman, president and director of the Foreign Policy Research Institute, is the author of such books as *America the Vulnerable: Our Military Problems and How to Fix Them* (2002) and *Palestinian Autonomy, Self-Government and Peace* (1993).

Introduction

by Dr. Harvey Sicherman

America's triumph in the Cold War promised a new burst of peace and prosperity. Indeed, the decade between the demise of the Soviet Union and the destruction of September 11, 2001, proved deceptively hopeful. Today, of course, we are more fully aware—to our sorrow—of the dangers and troubles no longer just below the surface.

The Muslim identities of most of the terrorists at war with the United States have also provoked great interest in Islam as well as the role of religion in politics. It is crucial for Americans not to assume that Osama bin Laden's ideas are identical to those of most Muslims or, for that matter, that most Muslims are Arabs. A truly world religion, Islam claims hundreds of millions of adherents, from every ethnic group scattered across the globe. This book series covers the growth and influence of Muslims in Asia and Central Asia.

A glance at the map establishes the extraordinary coverage of our authors. Every climate and terrain may be found, along with every form of human society, from the nomadic groups of the Central Asian steppes to highly sophisticated cities such as Singapore, New Delhi, and Shanghai. The

Eduardo Ermita, defense secretary of the Philippines, uses a chart to show reporters how the international terrorist organization al-Qaeda funneled money to a member of Jemaah Islamiyah, an Islamist organization that has carried out terrorist attacks across Asia.

economies of the nations examined in this series are likewise highly diverse. In some, barter systems are still used; others incorporate modern stock markets. In some of the countries, large oil reserves hold out the prospect of prosperity. Other countries, such as India and China, have progressed by moving from a government-controlled to a more market-based economic system. Still other countries have built wealth on service and shipping.

Central Asia and Asia is a heavily armed and turbulent area. Three of its states (China, India, and Pakistan) are nuclear powers, and one (Kazakhstan) only recently rid itself of nuclear weapons. But it is also a place where the horse and mule remain indispensable instruments of war. All of the region's states have an extensive history of conflict, domestic and international, old and new. Afghanistan, for example, has known little but invasion and civil war over the past two decades.

Governments include dictatorships, democracies, and hybrids without a name; centralized and decentralized administrations; and older patterns of tribal and clan associations. The region is a veritable encyclopedia of political expression.

Although such variety defies easy generalities, it is still possible to make several observations. First, the geopolitics of Central Asia and Asia reflect the impact of empires and the struggles of post-imperial independence. Central Asia, a historic corridor for traders and soldiers, was the scene of Russian expansion well into Soviet times. While Kazakhstan's leaders participated in the historic meeting of December 25, 1991, that dissolved the Soviet Union, the rest of the region's newly independent republics hardly expected it. They have found it difficult to grapple with a sometimes tenuous independence, buffeted by a strong residual Russian influence, the absence of settled institutions, the temptation of newly valuable natural resources, and mixed populations lacking a solid national identity. The shards of the Soviet Union have often been sharp—witness the Russian war in Chechnya—and sometimes fatal for those ambitious to grasp them.

Moving further east, one encounters an older devolution, that of the half-century since the British Raj dissolved into India and Pakistan (the latter giving violent birth to Bangladesh in 1971). Only recently, partly under the impact of the war on terrorism, have these nuclear-armed neighbors and adversaries found it possible to renew attempts at reconciliation. Still further east, Malaysia shares a British experience, but Indonesia has been influenced by its Dutch heritage. Even China defines its own borders along the lines of the Qing empire (the last pre-republican dynasty) at its most expansionist (including Tibet and Taiwan). These imperial histories lie heavily upon the politics of the region.

A second aspect worth noting is the variety of economic experimentation afoot in the area. State-dominated economic strategies, still in the ascendant, are separating government from the actual running of commerce and industry. "Privatization," however, is frequently a byword for crony capitalism and corruption. Yet in dynamic economies such as that of China, as well as an increasingly productive India, hundreds of millions of people have dramatically improved both their standard of living and their hope for the future. All of them aspire to benefit from international trade. Competitive advantages, such as low-cost labor (in some cases trained in high technology) and valuable natural resources (oil, gas, and minerals), promise much. This is indeed a revolution of rising expectations, some of which are being satisfied.

Yet more than corruption threatens this progress. Population increase, even though moderating, still overwhelms educational and employment opportunities. Many countries are marked by extremes of wealth and poverty, especially between rural and urban areas. Dangerous jealousies threaten ethnic groups (such as anti-Chinese violence in Indonesia). Hopelessly overburdened public services portend turmoil. Public health, never adequate, is harmed further by environmental damage to critical resources (such as the Aral Sea). By and large, Central Asian and Asian countries are living well beyond their infrastructures.

Third and finally, Islam has deeply affected the states and peoples of the region. Indonesia is the largest Muslim state in the world, and India hosts the second-largest Muslim population. Islam is not only the official religion of many states, it is the very reason for Pakistan's existence. But Islamic practices and groups vary: the well-known Sunni and Shiite groups are joined by energetic Salafi (Wahabi) and Sufi movements. Over the last 20 years especially, South and Central Asia have become battlegrounds for competing Shiite (Iranian) and Wahabi (Saudi) doctrines, well financed from abroad and aggressively antagonistic toward non-Muslims and each other. Resistance to the Soviet invasion of Afghanistan brought these groups battle-tested warriors and organizers. The war on terrorism has exposed just how far-reaching and active the new advocates of holy war (jihad) can be. Indonesia, in particular, is the scene of rivalry between an older, tolerant Islam and the jihadists. But Pakistan also faces an Islamic identity crisis. And India, wracked by sectarian strife, must hold together its democratic framework despite Muslim and Hindu extremists.

Two suspected al-Qaeda supporters behind bars in a prison in Wana, Pakistan. As part of its "war on terrorism"—launched in the aftermath of the September 11, 2001, attacks on New York and Washington—the United States has encouraged and prodded the governments of Asian countries to crack down on Islamic extremists in their midst.

This newly significant struggle within Islam, superimposed on an older Muslim history, will shape political and economic destinies throughout the region and beyond. Hence, the focus of our series.

We hope that these books will enlighten both teacher and student about a critical subject in a critical area of the world. Central Asia and Asia would be important in their own right to Americans; arguably, after 9/11, they became vital to our national security. And the enduring impact of Islam is a crucial factor we must understand. We at the Foreign Policy Research Institute hope these books will illuminate both the facts and the prospects.

An Indian Muslim performs his morning prayers. With an estimated 1.3 billion adherents worldwide, Islam claims more followers than any other religion except Christianity.

Overview: Islam in Asia

Covering nearly 30 percent of earth's total land area, Asia is by far the largest continent. It is also the most populous, serving as home to more than half of the world's people. In fact, of the world's 10 most populous countries, 6 lie entirely within Asia. In addition to the two largest, China and India (each of which claims more than 1 billion inhabitants), these include Indonesia, Pakistan, Bangladesh, and Japan.

Asia is generally divided into four main regions: South Asia, Southeast Asia, East Asia, and Central Asia. South Asia is composed of Pakistan, India, Sri Lanka, the Maldives, Bangladesh, and Nepal. Southeast Asia includes Indonesia, the Philippines, Malaysia, Thailand, Myanmar (formerly Burma),

Cambodia, and Vietnam. East Asia contains North and South Korea, Taiwan, Japan, and most of China. Central Asia includes western China, Afghanistan, and the former Soviet republics of the region: Turkmenistan, Uzbekistan, Tajikistan, Kyrgyzstan, and Kazakhstan. (Although Russia occupies the largest Asian territory, its culture and people are mostly European, and thus it is typically not included in discussions of Asia. Similarly, Turkey is classified as a European country even though it takes up a good portion of southwestern Asia, and Iran, while geographically part of Central Asia, is more often discussed in the context of the greater Middle East. The Asian part of the Middle East is not covered in this book or series.)

Asia is a continent of enormous geographic diversity. It contains some of the world's largest and driest deserts, including the Taklamakan in China and the Gobi in Mongolia. It also features the highest mountains on the planet, the Himalayas, as well as some of the most powerful rivers, such as the Yangtze, Mekong, and Ganges.

Asia's greatest diversity, however, is found among its peoples, which include groups of Mongoloid stock in China and East Asia; Malay peoples in Southeast Asia; Negritos in Malaysia and the Philippines; Indo-Aryans in India and Sri Lanka; and **Turkic** populations throughout Central Asia. Stone Age customs endure among isolated tribes in Indonesia's Irian Jaya and India's Andaman and Nicobar Islands, while the South Koreans and Japanese are among the world's leaders in the development and use of cell phones and other forms of modern technology.

Religion in Asia: Coexistence and Conflict

Asia is also a place of great religious diversity where virtually all of the world's major faiths are practiced. But Islam is the official or predominant religion of more Asian countries than any other faith. It is the majority religion in Turkmenistan, Uzbekistan, Tajikistan, Kyrgyzstan, Kazakhstan, Pakistan, Afghanistan, Bangladesh, Indonesia, Malaysia, and the

Maldives. (The *-stan* ending in many of these countries' names means "country" or "region" in Persian, the language of Iran. It is used to designate both modern states and regions with clear ethnic and geographic identities—Waziristan, for example, is a largely tribal autonomous region in western Pakistan.)

In other Asian countries, Islam claims about the same number of adherents as other major faiths, or it is practiced by a minority. In many countries of East and Southeast Asia, Islam or Buddhism coexists with Christianity. The Philippines are primarily Roman Catholic, for example, although a significant and growing Muslim minority lives in the country's southern islands.

Sri Lanka, Thailand, Nepal, Myanmar, and Japan are largely Buddhist (Japanese people also practice the ancient Shinto religion); the tribal peoples of Southeast Asia are **animist**; and India is predominantly Hindu. However, Indian Muslims, though a minority, number more than 125 million—12 percent of the total population—which makes India the world's third-largest Muslim country, behind Indonesia and Pakistan. Singapore, Thailand, and Cambodia also have significant Muslim populations (5 percent or more) that are growing.

In addition to the major faiths, there are some religions in Asia whose adherents number only in the tens or hundreds of thousands. These include Zoroastrianism, Bahaism, and Ismailism (an unorthodox version of Islam).

As membership in some religions wanes, other faiths are gaining adherents by spreading into countries where they were previously unknown or had only modest followings. Christianity's Protestant denominations have made major inroads in South Korea; Islam is gaining ground in the Philippines, Indonesia, and Cambodia; and Roman Catholicism is winning followers in India—a development that has moved Hindu nationalists to call for restrictions on Catholics.

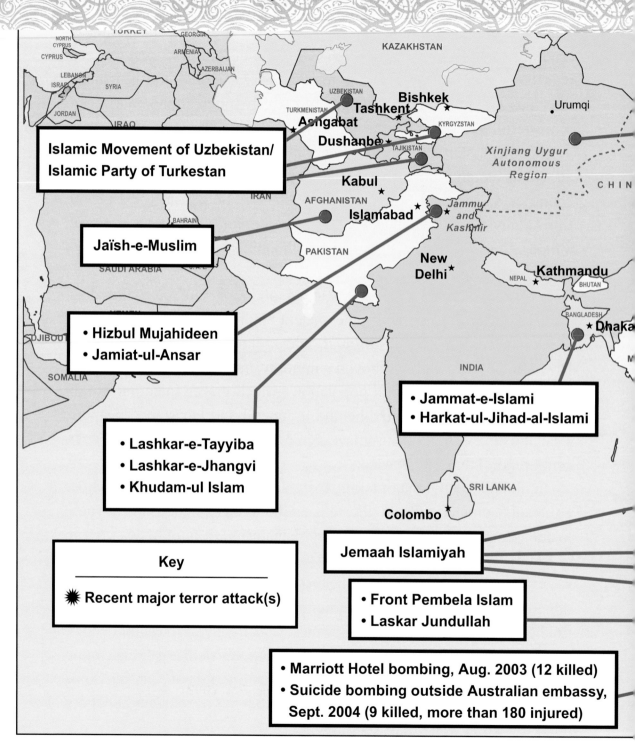

Islamic Movement of Uzbekistan/ Islamic Party of Turkestan

Jaïsh-e-Muslim

- **Hizbul Mujahideen**
- **Jamiat-ul-Ansar**

- **Lashkar-e-Tayyiba**
- **Lashkar-e-Jhangvi**
- **Khudam-ul Islam**

- **Jammat-e-Islami**
- **Harkat-ul-Jihad-al-Islami**

Key

✹ **Recent major terror attack(s)**

Jemaah Islamiyah

- **Front Pembela Islam**
- **Laskar Jundullah**

- **Marriott Hotel bombing, Aug. 2003 (12 killed)**
- **Suicide bombing outside Australian embassy, Sept. 2004 (9 killed, more than 180 injured)**

KAZAKHSTAN

NORTH CYPRUS
CYPRUS
LEBANON
ISRAEL
JORDAN
SYRIA
TURKEY
GEORGIA
ARMENIA
AZERBAIJAN

UZBEKISTAN
TURKMENISTAN
Ashgabat
Dushanbe
TAJIKISTAN

Tashkent
Bishkek
KYRGYZSTAN

Urumqi

Xinjiang Uygur Autonomous Region

CHINA

IRAQ

IRAN

AFGHANISTAN
Kabul

Islamabad

PAKISTAN

Jammu and Kashmir

SAUDI ARABIA

BAHRAIN

U.A.E.

New Delhi

NEPAL
Kathmandu
BHUTAN

BANGLADESH
★ **Dhaka**

DJIBOUTI

SOMALIA

YEMEN

INDIA

SRI LANKA

Colombo

Islamic Terrorist Groups

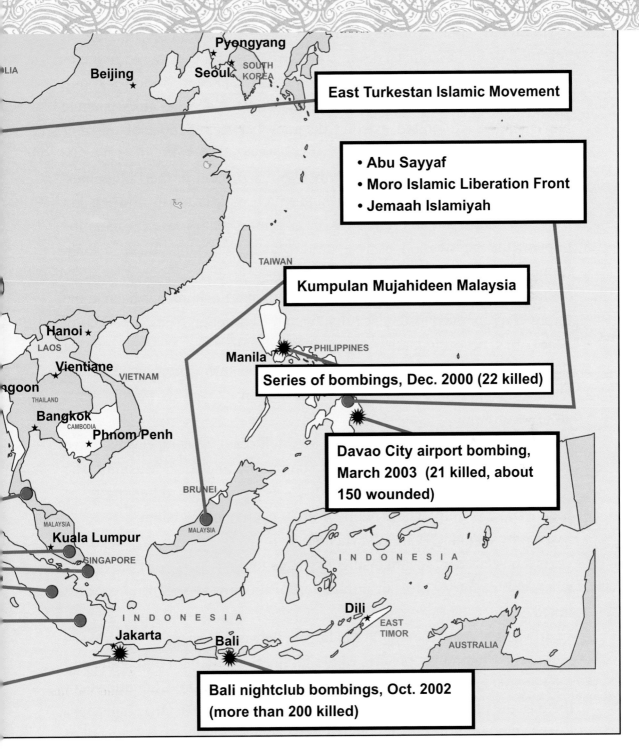

East Turkestan Islamic Movement

• Abu Sayyaf
• Moro Islamic Liberation Front
• Jemaah Islamiyah

Kumpulan Mujahideen Malaysia

Series of bombings, Dec. 2000 (22 killed)

Davao City airport bombing, March 2003 (21 killed, about 150 wounded)

Bali nightclub bombings, Oct. 2002 (more than 200 killed)

Interfaith relations in Asia can be relatively peaceful, as they are in several East and Southeast Asian countries; tense, as they are in India; or violent, as shown by present-day conflicts in Tajikistan, Indonesia, and the Philippines. Typically, these conflicts take place because Islamist movements have ignited existing disputes between people of different regions, cultures, or ethnicities.

Although Muslims constitute only about 5 percent of the Philippines' overall population, on southern islands such as Mindanao and Basilan they make up a sizeable minority or, in certain places, even a majority. Support for the creation of a separate Muslim state has fueled a long-running insurgency.

India's only Muslim-majority state, Jammu and Kashmir, has been in the throes of a separatist insurgency that, with the exception of short periods of peace, has been simmering since 1947. Because the Muslim state of Pakistan also claims Jammu and Kashmir, the insurgency has received financial support and manpower from Pakistan as well as from Islamist groups worldwide.

On Indonesia's Maluku Islands (or Moluccas), violent clashes have erupted between the large Christian community and local Muslims. The latter have received support from co-religionists in other parts of Indonesia, a country where nearly 9 in 10 people follow Islam.

Nearby Thailand is an overwhelmingly Buddhist country. Yet in recent years it has faced a Muslim insurgency in its four southernmost provinces, where the country's Muslim population of roughly 4 percent is concentrated.

In Central Asia, the conflict is largely between a *secular* elite that is heir to the Communist policies of the former Soviet Union and a growing segment of citizens returning to the Islamic faith of the pre-Communist era (before the 1920s). Tensions are greatest in Uzbekistan, Tajikistan, Kyrgyzstan, and Kazakhstan, which were Soviet republics until the fall of the Soviet Union in 1991.

China also faces a restive Muslim population in its extreme northwestern region of Xinjiang (also spelled Sinkiang). A vast, largely desolate land, Xinjiang is inhabited mostly by ethnic Uygurs—a Turkic-speaking people also present in Kyrgyzstan and Kazakhstan, as well as in Mongolia. The Uygurs have little in common with the Han Chinese, who make up some 92 percent of China's population and dominate the government and culture. In recent years the Chinese government has blamed Uygur separatists for several bombings and other acts of terrorism.

The Founding and Spread of Islam

In number of adherents, Islam is the second-largest religion (behind only Christianity). Estimates place the number of Muslims worldwide at about 1.3 billion.

A replica of a ninth-century Arab dhow, or trading vessel, drops anchor in Singapore's harbor. Islam spread into East Asia largely through the activities of traders and missionaries, rather than through conquest, as was the case in other parts of the world.

The beginning of the Islamic era is conventionally dated to A.D. 622, the year the prophet Muhammad (ca. 570–632) and his followers were forced to leave the city of Mecca (in present-day Saudi Arabia) for the oasis town of Yathrib (now known as Medina). Muslims believe that a dozen years earlier, in 610, Muhammad received the first in a series of life-long revelations from Allah, or God. Some time after, he began preaching

Allah's message—the essence of which is that there is only one God and that the righteous must submit to His will. This drew the ire of wealthy and powerful Meccans, not only because they were polytheistic but also because they profited from the pilgrims who flocked to their city to worship the idols at a shrine known as the Kaaba.

After the flight from Mecca, Muhammad and his followers—now known as Muslims, from a word meaning "one who submits" (to God)—established an Islamic society in Medina. They staved off several Meccan military expeditions and, by 630, had defeated their enemy and returned triumphantly to Mecca. Most Meccans willingly converted to Islam at that time.

In the decades following Muhammad's death in 632, Islam spread quickly beyond the Arabian Peninsula. Like Christianity and unlike Judaism, Islam is a missionary, or evangelical, religion—it seeks to gain converts. Initially Islam was spread mainly by the sword, as Muslim armies swept through the Middle East, North Africa, and, by the second decade of the eighth century, Spain. Muslims would later conquer Central Asia, northern India, southeastern Europe's Balkan Peninsula, and parts of sub-Saharan Africa, in the process spreading their faith into these regions.

Islam's spread into East and Southeast Asia occurred through more peaceful means, particularly trade and missionary work. Muslim merchants, sailors, and missionaries from Yemen and Oman—located on the Arabian Peninsula—carried their faith eastward along sea routes. Over the course of centuries, some of the East and Southeast Asians who came into contact with these Arabs began to adopt their religion.

One consequence of the voluntary and gradual adoption of Islam in East and Southeast Asia was that the form of the religion practiced in those regions tended to be highly **syncretic**—in other words, it accepted and included elements of pre-Islamic religious beliefs (such as animism,

Buddhism, and Hinduism). Asian Muslims also were—and, in fact, continue to be—more tolerant of other religious faiths than their Middle Eastern or North African counterparts (although the situation has begun to change in the present era as fundamentalists have gained more influence). Today Muslim missionaries are still active in Asia, funded greatly by Saudi Arabia and other oil-producing Persian Gulf states.

Major Sects of Islam

As Christians belong to various churches with somewhat differing beliefs and practices (Roman Catholic, Eastern Orthodox, assorted Protestant denominations), Muslims are divided into two major branches—the **Sunni** and the **Shia**, or Shiites—each claiming to be the legitimate voice of Islam and asserting that the other has deviated from the true path. In addition, a number of smaller Islamic sects exist, both within and outside the two major branches.

The Sunni (from the Arabic *Sunnah*, meaning "custom," "method," "path," or "example") is by far the larger of Islam's two major branches: some 80 percent of Muslims worldwide are Sunnis. Shiites, by contrast, make up only about 15 percent of Muslims overall (although they constitute a majority in certain countries, such as Iran, Iraq, and Bahrain).

In many areas of Asia, Islamic traditions were fused with the practices and rituals of earlier religions. A pre-Islamic gong is used to accompany the traditional Muslim call to prayer in this mosque in Demak, Indonesia.

Although there are differences between the Sunni and Shia branches of Islam, all devout Muslims observe five practices, known as the Five Pillars of Islam, as basic obligations of their faith. One of these is the pilgrimage to the holy city of Mecca, called the hajj, which all Muslims are supposed to make at least once in their lifetime if they are able. Here, faithful Muslims surround the Kaaba, an ancient shrine in Mecca, during the annual hajj.

Although today the Sunni and Shia differ on many theological and ritual issues (and have a long history of strained relations), the roots of their rift lie with a practical matter from Islam's early years. Upon Muhammad's death in 632, the question arose as to who should assume the role of caliph, or successor to the Prophet as temporal and spiritual leader of the Muslim community. The Sunnis believed that the caliph should be elected by tribal chiefs. No, said the Shiites (the term derives from *shi'at Ali*, "the party of Ali"), succession should follow the bloodline of Ali ibn Abi Talib. Ali was the Prophet's cousin and son-in-law, having married Muhammad's daughter Fatima. (Muhammad himself had no sons who survived to adulthood.) But the Sunni view prevailed, and Ali was passed over three times before finally becoming Islam's fourth caliph, in 656. He was assassinated five years later.

The Sunni majority itself is divided into the followers of four distinct schools of *fiqh*, or Islamic jurisprudence: Hanafi, Shafii, Maliki, and Hanbali. These schools of thought, developed during the eighth and ninth centuries, provided legal opinions from Islamic scholars on what was desirable or permissible for Muslims in various situations not explicitly dealt with in the **Qur'an** (Islam's holy book). The four schools vary somewhat in the way in which they arrive at rulings, and in their relative liberality or restrictiveness. But each is recognized as equally legitimate and "orthodox" by nearly all Sunni Muslims, with the notable exception of the **Wahhabis**, who ascribe sole authority to the Hanbali school.

Named after its founder, Muhammad ibn Abd al-Wahab (ca. 1703–1791), the Wahhabi sect emerged during the 18th century in what is today Saudi Arabia. Al-Wahab sought to return Islam to its earliest form by cleansing the religion of what he regarded as un-Islamic practices that had arisen over the centuries (for example, the Shiites' veneration of saints). Wahhabis believe that only a literal reading of the Qur'an can provide the basis for **Sharia**, or Islamic law; they reject as illegitimate the *fiqh*

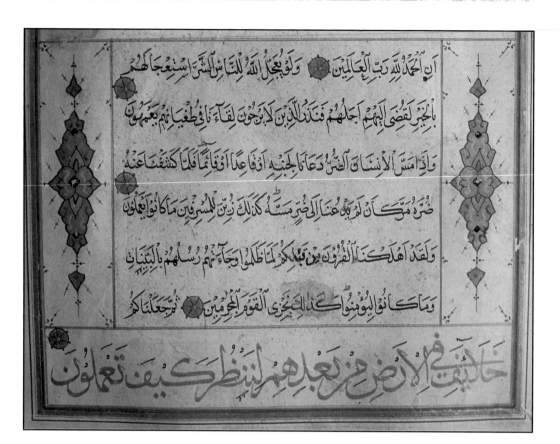

An ornate page from the Qur'an, Islam's holy scriptures. Islamists believe that a rigid, literal reading of the Qur'an should be the basis for all government.

schools' use of analogy or consensus among scholars to determine what is permissible for Muslims. Wahhabism, which is dominant in Saudi Arabia, has inspired fundamentalist movements in other countries, most famously among the ***Taliban*** of Afghanistan, who were in power from 1996 to 2001. However, because Wahhabism has negative connotations, most Muslims who embrace the tenets of the sect do not refer to themselves as Wahhabis.

In the centuries after the initial schism between the Sunnis and the minority Shia, important theological differences emerged. In addition, the role of the clergy in Islam's two main branches developed along distinct lines. The Shia clergy—particularly the learned and respected leaders known as ayatollahs—acquired much more authority. Unlike the Sunni clergy, who have no universally recognized center of worldly authority, the Shia ayatollahs, centered in the holy cities of Najaf and Karbala in Iraq and Qum in Iran, are actively involved in making decisions in the political as well as religious sphere. In Iran, the world's only country that is politically dominated by Shia, ultimate power rests with the ayatollahs.

International Islamist groups and governments may find support from Shia as well as Sunni sources—Iranian oil money funds many Islamist networks, for example—but virtually all Islamist terrorist groups are Sunni. Some of these groups, such as Lashkar-e-Jhangvi in Pakistan, list among their stated goals the elimination of Shias, whom they see as heretics and betrayers of the "true" Islam.

In religiously tolerant Asia, where Islam coexisted peacefully with other faiths for many centuries, a fundamentalist outlook has emerged in recent decades with the growing influence of the Wahhabis and the Shias. Since the 1970s, a Wahhabi global network has developed, from Bosnia to Pakistan, thanks in large part to the expanding oil wealth of Saudi Arabia and other Sunni Muslim nations of OPEC (the Organization of Petroleum Exporting Countries). While competing with the Shias of Iran, extremist Sunnis have actively exported their interpretations to poorer countries in Asia, attracting ambitious young people to their Islamic universities. As a result, a more militant and violent understanding of Islam has become more prevalent in many Asian countries. This understanding has been encouraged, if not created, by Arab- or Iranian-trained clerics.

An Indonesian soldier walks through the rubble of a Bali nightclub destroyed by a massive car bomb, October 2002. The attack, which killed more than 200 people, was linked to the Islamist terrorist group Jemaah Islamiyah.

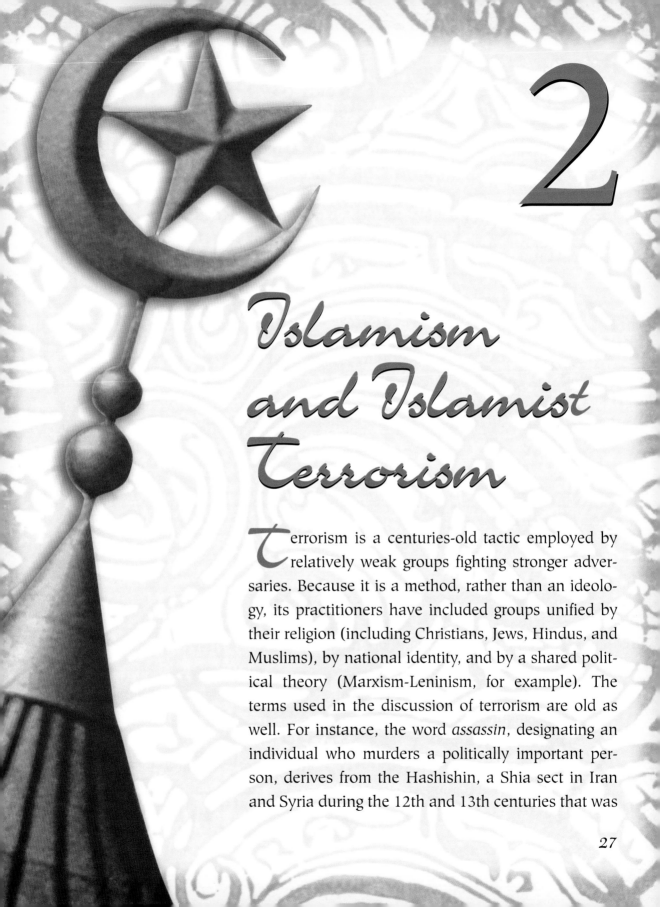

2

Islamism and Islamist Terrorism

Terrorism is a centuries-old tactic employed by relatively weak groups fighting stronger adversaries. Because it is a method, rather than an ideology, its practitioners have included groups unified by their religion (including Christians, Jews, Hindus, and Muslims), by national identity, and by a shared political theory (Marxism-Leninism, for example). The terms used in the discussion of terrorism are old as well. For instance, the word *assassin*, designating an individual who murders a politically important person, derives from the Hashishin, a Shia sect in Iran and Syria during the 12th and 13th centuries that was said to use hashish to train its fighters to carry out their attacks without hesitation.

Although the phenomenon of terrorism is both old and widely distributed across cultures and regions, the word *terrorism* confounds attempts at precise definition. In fact, there is today no internationally established consensus over how to define the term. A working definition that will suffice for the purposes of this book is "the use or threat of violence against civilian or noncombatant targets, with the political purpose of changing government policies or institutions." Under this definition, terrorism can be distinguished from other acts of violence or intimidation by the characteristics of the victims and by the motivations of the perpetrators.

Terrorism, according to the definition offered above, targets people who are not actively engaged in warfare. Typically this means civilians, but under certain circumstances military personnel could also be victims of terrorism. In 1983, for example, a suicide bomber drove an explosive-laden truck into the U.S. Marine barracks in Beirut, Lebanon, killing more than 240 American servicemen. Because the Marines were in Beirut as peacekeepers rather than as combatants, the attack would be considered an act of terrorism. Used by, say, an Iraqi soldier against a Marine unit during the U.S. invasion of Iraq, the identical tactic would not be regarded as terrorism but as an act of war.

Terrorism is committed for political ends—to coerce governments to alter their policies, to intimidate societies into changing their institutions or modifying their activities. It should be readily apparent that this political motivation is what distinguishes the terrorist from, for example, the serial murderer—even though each might enact deadly violence on random civilians.

It should also be noted that, according to many definitions, terrorism can only be committed by what the U.S. State Department refers to as "subnational actors." In other words, the acts of states cannot be said to

Islamist extremists do not have a monopoly on terrorism. In fact, many groups and peoples have used terrorism throughout history to help achieve their political goals. These masked men, pictured circa 1972, are members of the Ulster Defense Association, a paramilitary group that clashed in Northern Ireland with another terrorist group, the Irish Republican Army.

constitute terrorism—even when those acts represent violence against civilians and are designed to change the policies of another government. However, states can sponsor terrorist groups.

A terrorist group is defined as any organization whose main method of action is terrorism. This is not to suggest that such groups necessarily employ only terrorism in the pursuit of their goals. Sometimes a terrorist group is affiliated with a legal or illegal political party, serving as the party's armed wing; sometimes an organization that engages in terrorism also provides humanitarian aid or social services through an associated non-governmental organization (NGO).

International terrorism is terrorism perpetrated by groups operating in more than one country. For several years, the world's most notorious international terror network has been **al-Qaeda**, the organization that planned and executed the plane attacks in New York and Washington, D.C., on September 11, 2001.

Islamist terrorists belong to many distinct groups with different agendas, but they generally share a commitment to wage *jihad* (holy war) and the desire to establish a worldwide Islamic state, or **caliphate**. Asian Islamist groups seek the same goal, and they are all linked in some manner to a worldwide revival of Islamism, which originated in Egypt and Pakistan and is centered today in Pakistan and Saudi Arabia. Until the end of 2001 and the U.S. attack on the Taliban regime in Afghanistan, that country served as the primary center for global Islamist terrorist training and planning.

In any discussion of this subject, it must be pointed out that while Islamist terrorism has enjoyed growing worldwide support, it is still a means used by a small minority of Muslims, and the level of support for terrorists varies from country to country. Most of the world's 1.3 billion Muslims are neither terrorists nor supportive of terrorism. Furthermore, Islam as defined by mainstream theologians and practiced by the majority of Muslims is in no way a "terrorist" religion.

The Rise of Islamism in Asia

Islamism—which refers broadly to a fundamentalist political ideology that seeks to return Muslim societies to an earlier, supposed golden age in the history of Islam, with compulsory adherence to Sharia—does not necessarily imply the use of violence. Yet Islamic terrorism has frequently accompanied Islamism.

Although Islamism itself has taken a somewhat different form and arisen under varying circumstances in different regions of Asia (or even

The Ideology of al-Qaeda

Al-Qaeda's highly influential ideology is based on three basic premises:

1) that modern Western values, influence, and culture are a threat to true Islam;

2) that the worldwide Muslim community, or **umma**, has strayed from God; and

3) that the only solution is for the **umma** to return to a strict and literal interpretation of Islam based on Sharia, or Islamic law.

The short-lived Taliban regime in Afghanistan was seen as the closest model to the perfect Islamic society sought by al-Qaeda.

different countries within the same region), it is possible to identify certain key events in the recent spread of this ideology. In early 1979, capitalizing on popular discontent with the U.S.-backed shah, the Shia cleric Ayatollah Ruhollah Khomeini led a successful revolution and set up a conservative Islamic **theocracy** in Iran. Soon after, Iran began trying to export its conservative Islamic revolution to other parts of the Muslim world. In December 1979, partly to forestall the possibility of an Iranian-style Islamist regime coming to power along the southern border of its Central Asian republics, the Soviet Union invaded Afghanistan. The Soviet invasion and occupation of Afghanistan, in turn, galvanized Afghans as well as other Muslims, particularly Arabs. A significant number of Arabs joined the fight against the Soviets in Afghanistan, and for many the decade-long struggle helped solidify a powerful Islamist worldview, which they would later seek to spread. In addition, many young Afghan refugees in Pakistan

The Ayatollah Khomeini greets his supporters after returning to Iran in February 1979. The radical cleric inspired a revolution that toppled the authoritarian regime of Iran's shah, replacing it with the equally authoritarian rule of conservative Shiite Muslim leaders.

received a Wahhabi-inspired education (funded by Saudi Arabia); after returning to Afghanistan following the Soviet withdrawal in 1989, these students would form the core of the Islamist Taliban regime.

When the Soviet Union collapsed in 1991, its Central Asian republics—Uzbekistan, Turkmenistan, Kazakhstan, Tajikistan, and Kyrgyzstan—gained their independence. These lands were historically Muslim, but Islam (and all other religions) had been aggressively repressed by the officially atheistic Soviet Communists. The end of Soviet rule was accompanied by a broad religious revival. But the leaders of the newly independent Central Asian states were reluctant to embrace this upsurge in Islamic faith and practice—not only because they were all former Soviet officials who had been indoctrinated in the atheism of the Communist Party, but also because they saw Islam as a potential threat to their authority. The Central Asian leaders generally tried to control the practice of Islam in their countries or to adapt it to their own political purposes. When those attempts failed, they tended to adopt more repressive measures. This was—and still is—especially the case in the largest of the former Soviet republics of Central Asia, Uzbekistan. There the government prohibits all Islamic practice except in the context of carefully monitored state-sanctioned **mosques**.

But controlling Islam, and Islamism, has proved difficult in the post-Soviet era. Perhaps because their own religious traditions had long been repressed, Central Asians after 1991 were open to outside influences, particularly the Wahhabist school. With funding from Saudi Arabia and other Persian Gulf states, Central Asian Muslims began to build new mosques and undergo training in Saudi Arabia to become **imams**. They also built ties with their regional neighbor Afghanistan. Developments in Afghanistan had a clear and lasting influence over Islam in the newly independent Central Asian states. The Afghan **mujahideen**, freedom fighters who resisted the Soviet occupation of 1979–89, became heroes in the eyes of many

Russians protest outside the Kremlin, September 1991. By the end of that year, the Soviet Union had disintegrated, and its predominantly Muslim republics in Central Asia had gained their independence.

of the region's Muslims. Some Central Asians—especially Uzbeks—joined the Taliban movement that emerged in Afghanistan after the Soviet withdrawal, and some became part of the al-Qaeda organization. One group with links to al-Qaeda and the Taliban is the Islamic Movement of Uzbekistan (IMU), now known as the Islamic Party of Turkestan (IPT). Members of this extremist organization, which seeks the establishment of a Muslim state in Central Asia and is active in Uzbekistan, Kazakhstan, Tajikistan, and Kyrgyzstan, fought alongside al-Qaeda and Taliban forces against the U.S.-led coalition that invaded Afghanistan in 2001 following the terrorist attacks of September 11.

Islamist Ideology

While there are many different Islamist groups around the world, they share a common belief that the only period of "pure" Islamic life was early in the development of the faith (for example, during the reign of the first four caliphs). Islamist groups also share the goals of recovering "authentic" Islam and restoring the characteristics of the faith in its supposed golden age. In that endeavor, the following goals are considered most crucial: 1) eliminating all non-Islamic, especially Christian and Jewish, influences in the Islamic world; 2) re-creating a worldwide caliphate, or Islamic state; 3) recovering all the territories that were ever under Islamic occupation (including the Iberian Peninsula, Sicily, Crete, most of the Balkans, and most of India); 4) applying a strict interpretation of Islamic law for all Muslims everywhere; 5) overthrowing governments in Muslim-majority countries that do not accept and apply these conditions; and 6) embarking on a holy war to enforce these goals.

Islamists draw from old traditions of scholarship to inform their rhetoric. The oldest of the ideological sources of Islamist radicalism, popular in Asia and beyond, is the Deobandi school of thought. The school's influence is widespread in Pakistan and Central Asia (the Taliban were Deobandis) and even reaches Muslims in Western Europe, especially in the United Kingdom. The movement, which originated in India, derived its name from the town of Deoband, 90 miles (145 km) northeast of New Delhi. The *maulana* (cleric) Mohamed Qasim Nanotyi founded Darul Uloom (House of Knowledge), the Deobandis' first learning center, in 1866. Many of the school's teachers were veterans of the 1857 independence conflict known as the Indian Mutiny. In that conflict, Muslims joined with Hindus in resisting British rule, but they were unsuccessful. The Darul Uloom's founders established the school in opposition to the British ban on Muslim education.

Today Darul Uloom is the world's second-largest center of Sunni Islamic study, after Al-Azhar University in Cairo, Egypt. Thousands of students have completed their schooling at Darul Uloom, most around the age of 25, and many have gone on to establish and run **madrassas**—Islamic schools—in Pakistan and Afghanistan.

One of the most controversial aspects of the Deobandi school is its attitude toward women. Women, Deobandis teach, must wear veils or **burkas** and cannot socialize with unrelated men outside the home. Because girls are considered less intelligent than boys, they are not to be educated past the age of eight. Students at Darul Uloom also may not use the Internet or watch movies, and in many Deobandi madrassas outside India, television and newspapers are banned altogether, as are all other forms of entertainment.

While some Deobandi graduates have embraced a life of violence, Darul Uloom does not openly encourage its students in this direction. However, Deobandi schools do exhort students to purge themselves of Western and modern influences. In India they have preached for the end of syncretic practices, such as combining Muslim rituals with Hindu traditions like the worship of idols.

Although Deobandi Muslims in India remain largely apolitical and ostensibly loyal to the Indian government, Deobandi ideology teaches that a Muslim's first allegiance must be to Islam, and national authority (or even national borders) takes a backseat to the needs of the *umma,* the worldwide community of Muslims. Deobandis believe that they have a right—even a duty—to wage jihad in defense of fellow Muslims in any country, and Deobandi ideology has motivated its students to engage in terrorism, especially in Pakistan and Bangladesh, neighboring countries of India. One of the most important Deobandi scholars and proponents of Islamism, Sayed Abu Ala Maududi (1903–79), was the founder of Pakistan's Jamaat-e-Islami. His ideas remain an inspiration for Pakistani Islamist terror groups today.

The dome and minaret of a mosque at Darul Uloom University look out over the town of Deoband, India. This famous center of learning is the oldest source of Islamist ideology.

Another major source of Islamist ideology is **Salafism**. While its origins lie in the Middle East, this movement and school of thought cannot be overlooked in a discussion of Asian Islamism. Among Islamists worldwide, Salafism has the largest following, and its proponents have the most financial resources. It also is the most organized movement in the majority of predominantly Muslim countries. There are several offshoots of Salafism, but the common goal among its followers is to remain loyal to the ways of the prophet Muhammad and his immediate successors.

The Egyptian scholar Sayyid Qutb (1906–1966) was a prominent leader of the modern Salafi movement and a spokesman for the most important—and still most influential—Islamist organization: the Muslim Brotherhood (al-Ikhwan al-Muslimoon). The Muslim Brotherhood is, ideologically, the mother lode of all Islamist terror organizations, and Sayyid Qutb—who was hanged for plotting to overthrow the Egyptian government—is their ultimate philosophical guide.

Founded in Egypt in the 1920s to revive Islam in the Middle East in the face of growing Western influences after World War I, the Muslim Brotherhood saw Islam as "creed and state, book and sword, and a way of life." The Brotherhood was banned in many Muslim countries, but it continued to grow under its first leader, Hassan al-Banna, who established the group's creed in 1949.

Hassan al-Banna (1906–1949) founded the Muslim Brotherhood, the most important and influential Salafist organization, in Egypt during the late 1920s.

Today the Muslim Brotherhood has branches, under various names, in more than 70 countries all over the world. However, all Brotherhood groups share the common goals of following the teachings and example of the Salaf (Islam's early leaders); rejecting any action or principle that contradicts the Qur'an or Sunna (the example of the prophet Muhammad and his companions); promoting Islamic government and law; and establishing a caliphate among Islamic states. Their motto is "Allah is our objective, the messenger is our leader, Qur'an is our law, Jihad is our way, and Dying in the way of Allah is our highest hope."

The Role of Education

The spread of Islamic fundamentalism—and, more specifically, the indoctrination of potential terrorist recruits—has been greatly facilitated by the operation of certain madrassas (also spelled madrassahs), especially in Pakistan, Bangladesh, and Indonesia. In thousands of these Islamic schools, often funded by money from Saudi Arabia or other oil-rich Persian Gulf states, boys (in most places girls are not allowed to study) as young as six years of age are offered a free education. However, instruction is often limited to learning Arabic (usually not the students' first language) and reciting the Qur'an by heart. There is little, if any, education in subjects such as history, geography, math, or "Western" science, and the teachers in these madrassas are often themselves poorly educated. But because free public schools do not exist in some South and East Asian countries, and because the madrassas provide room and board, many poor parents feel that these Islamic schools offer the only chance for their sons to receive an education. Unfortunately, students as young as 10 are actively recruited as Islamic militants in some of these madrassas.

An article published in the *Christian Science Monitor* in August 2004 helped illustrate how madrassas serve as the ideological foundation of Islamism. The article's author, Owais Tohid, described a visit to a school in the small town of Gujar Khan, 35 miles (56 kilometers) from Islamabad, Pakistan's capital city. Tohid observed pupils seated on the floor and swaying as they recited the Qur'an under the watchful eye of their instructor. The teacher, who threatened to correct any errors by waving a tree branch at them, explained the students' role and his mission: "These are parrots of heaven. We teach our students purely Islamic teachings to make them pure and ideal Muslims who will not hesitate to sacrifice their lives for the cause of Islam."

At the time Tohid wrote his article, there were more than 20,000 madrassas in Pakistan alone, and just 300 or so offered lessons in subjects like math, science, and computers (and that minimal reform had been made only in response to government pressure to broaden the curriculum in exchange for U.S. aid). One Pakistani educator, Tauseef Ahmed, explained succinctly how madrassas in his country produce militants ready to answer the call to wage jihad. "Most madrassahs," Ahmed said, "do not impart military training or education, but they brainwash the students, and that is more dangerous. The habits can be changed, but not the souls. The fairy tales of these students come from the battlefield. Thus characters like Osama [bin Laden] and Mullah Omar [leader of the Taliban] are their heroes."

The Pakistan experience is far from unique; it is largely replicated in many Asian countries. Notable exceptions include China and the former Soviet republics of Central Asia, where education is a state monopoly and madrassas, other than the very few specifically and officially approved for preparing clerics, are banned.

The influence of madrassas in propagating Islamic extremism is perhaps best illustrated by the Taliban. *Taliban* is the Arabic plural of *talib* (Islamic student). True to the group's name, all of its leaders, along with many of their followers, were trained in Saudi-funded, Wahhabi-controlled madrassas for Afghan Pashtun refugees living in Pakistan during the 1980s.

Two young men study the Qur'an in a madrassa in Peshawar, Pakistan. For the most part, these Islamic schools are supported by donations from Saudi Arabia and staffed by Wahhabi Muslims, who teach their strict brand of Islam. Moderate Muslims complain that young madrassa students are brainwashed, making them easy recruits for militant Islamic groups.

When the Taliban fought their way to power in Afghanistan following the Soviet withdrawal, they imposed an extremely conservative, repressive Islamist agenda that had been instilled by their earlier madrassa training.

In addition, the Taliban played a crucial role in the training of Muslim terrorists from all over the world, including Asia, the Middle East, and even Western Europe and the United States. Before the fall of the Taliban regime in late 2001, some 20,000 Muslims from a variety of extremist groups went through al-Qaeda's terrorist training camps in Afghanistan. In addition to their training in the techniques of terrorism, all of these *jihadis* were indoctrinated in the Salafi version of Islam.

The Influence of al-Qaeda

Al-Qaeda may be the most familiar Islamist terrorist organization, largely because of its sponsorship of the September 11 attacks. Yet misconceptions about its structure persist among the general public. Contrary to popular belief, al-Qaeda is not a strictly hierarchical organization whose leaders—especially its founder, the Saudi millionaire Osama bin Laden—issue orders that are then carried out by subordinates. Rather, al-Qaeda is more of a strategic and ideological clearinghouse, inspiring Islamist terrorists and furthering discussion of general suggestions and goals but not necessarily taking the lead on operational planning or even providing funding. This has been the case especially since the U.S.-led invasion of Afghanistan ousted the Taliban and deprived bin Laden and other al-Qaeda leaders of their terrorist bases there. What continues to distinguish al-Qaeda from other terrorist networks is its internationalism: in the pursuit of its ultimate goal—reestablishing an Islamic caliphate as it imagines that caliphate existed between the 8th and 11th centuries—al-Qaeda has eliminated all national distinctions within its own ranks. Muslim extremists from Algeria, Morocco, Egypt, Indonesia, Pakistan, Yemen—even France, Great Britain, and the United States—have adopted al-Qaeda's mission as their own, making this organization truly global.

The roots of al-Qaeda lie in the fight against the Soviet occupation of Afghanistan. Around 1986, as a volunteer in the Afghan mujahideen's cause, Osama bin Laden—a civil engineer from one of Saudi Arabia's wealthiest families whose personal fortune has been estimated between $50 million and $300 million—established a training camp and gathered a nucleus of like-minded Arab fighters around him. The most important of these individuals was Ayman al-Zawahiri, who would become al-Qaeda's second-in-command and whom many analysts consider the organization's real visionary. A member of one of Egypt's most prominent families and a medical doctor by training, al-Zawahiri was the leader of Egyptian Islamic Jihad, an extremist group responsible for the 1981 assassination of Egyptian president Anwar Sadat (and, later, for the 1993 truck-bomb attack on the World Trade Center in New York). In 1989 bin Laden founded al-Qaeda ("the Base") to spread his vision for Islamic revival. From Afghanistan the organization, also known as the World Islamic Front for Jihad Against the Jews and Crusaders, expanded its operations throughout

Two of the world's most infamous terrorist leaders, Osama bin Laden (left) and his adviser Ayman al-Zawahiri. Their al-Qaeda terrorist network financed and helped plan numerous terrorist attacks, including the September 11, 2001, attacks on the World Trade Center and Pentagon in the United States.

the world, from the Middle East to Europe and New York.

Bin Laden's differences with the Saudi monarchy came to the fore in the wake of the 1991 Gulf War, which resulted in large numbers of U.S. military personnel ("infidels," in bin Laden's Wahabbist worldview) being stationed in Saudi Arabia, the birthplace of the Prophet. Eventually, the Saudi government revoked his citizenship. In 1992 bin Laden found sanctuary in Sudan, where by 1994 he was reportedly operating at least three terrorist training camps. After Sudan bowed to international pressure and expelled him in May 1996, bin Laden settled in Afghanistan, where the Taliban's rise to power was under way.

Throughout these early years al-Qaeda was a tightly knit organization, with an established hierarchy and clearly delineated roles for its various leaders. During its period in Afghanistan, bin Laden led a *shura* (council) that managed a network of training camps. Some camps trained terrorists who were based, born, or educated in Western countries and were planning to attack European and U.S. targets; others trained infantry fighters, many of whom joined the Taliban in 2001 to fight against the United States and the Northern Alliance, a coalition of anti-Taliban Afghans.

During the years that al-Qaeda was managing its training camps, it was also establishing formal and operational ties with Islamist organizations elsewhere. As a result, there are today dozens of groups with similar agendas—some independent, some related through finances, and some simply sharing al-Qaeda's ideology throughout the world. Because the connections with al-Qaeda and local organizations are so tenuous, it is difficult to blame al-Qaeda alone for specific attacks, at least since September 11, 2001.

After the rout of the Taliban and its supporters, al-Qaeda lost not only its facilities in Afghanistan, but also its leadership's ability to control and conduct foreign operations. (Bin Laden and al-Zawahiri, along with Taliban head Mullah Omar, escaped capture by U.S. and allied forces in late 2001; as of early 2005 the top al-Qaeda leaders were widely believed to be living somewhere along Pakistan's rugged, largely lawless border area with Afghanistan.)

In the aftermath of the Taliban's defeat, al-Qaeda became more dependent on associated foreign Islamist groups to carry out terrorist acts. It also adopted, or was forced to adopt, a decentralized structure, which, ironically, may actually work to its advantage. While the charismatic bin Laden and the highly intelligent al-Zawahiri continue to attract and inspire Islamist terrorists, al-Qaeda's new face as a network of ideologically related but often autonomous groups and cells is perhaps harder for governments to combat. And as al-Qaeda maintains a worldwide base of support without funding or controlling the smaller groups—including Indonesian (or indeed Southeast Asian) Jemaah Islamiyah (Islamic Society) and the Islamic Party of Turkestan—those groups are able to retain their own particular agendas. For its part, al-Qaeda appears committed to maintaining a highly ambitious ultimate goal: to create a fundamentalist Muslim empire, a new caliphate that will draw in every Muslim community throughout the world and include all Muslim areas, from Morocco to Indonesia and from Central Africa to Chechnya.

It is hard to describe precisely al-Qaeda's involvement in Asia because while many of its associates help to carry out al-Qaeda's agenda, they also pursue their own missions. For example, the Islamic Movement of Uzbekistan was actively involved in defending the Taliban in Afghanistan, but it has also followed its own goal of making Uzbekistan an Islamic state. For the sake of national security, most governments assume that al-Qaeda's terrorist targets, which have been mentioned in bin Laden's numerous public statements, are also shared by groups linked to al-Qaeda. These targets include the United States and Israel (and their main allies), China, India, Russia, Pakistan, and virtually all governments of Muslim-majority countries that, according to al-Qaeda, have betrayed the

U.S. soldiers patrol a mountainous area of Afghanistan, 2004. The United States responded to the September 11 attacks by invading Afghanistan, which was harboring al-Qaeda's leadership and providing training camps for the terrorist organization. This forced al-Qaeda to adopt a more decentralized, less hierarchical structure.

true precepts of Islam. (In this last category, the secular government of Turkey is most often mentioned.)

China, India, and Russia were chosen as targets because they are all accused of mistreating their Muslim populations. (In Russia terrorists are active in Chechnya, a subdivision where Muslims have waged a separatist revolt since 1994.) Pakistan was added to the list for collaborating with the United States in the so-called war on terror. Considering how many enemies are listed, it is not surprising that al-Qaeda and associated groups have operated on nearly every continent, or that they are under attack everywhere.

Jemaah Islamiyah

Though its international reach may not match that of al-Qaeda, Jemaah Islamiyah (JI) is one of the most important international Islamist terrorist organizations. Founded in Malaysia by two Indonesian Salafists of Yemeni origin, JI is a Southeast Asian organization with branches in Indonesia, Malaysia, Thailand, the Philippines, and Singapore. There are also marginal JI groups in Myanmar, Cambodia, and Australia.

Although it originated before al-Qaeda, JI has established such close ties and has such an ideological affinity with bin Laden's organization that in many ways it serves as al-Qaeda's arm in Southeast Asia. JI members were trained in al-Qaeda camps and fought in Afghanistan; Arabs have served as JI's leaders. These include Abu Bakar Ba'asyir, who was apprehended in 2003, and the late Abdullah Sungkar.

It is important to note that JI's interpretation of Islam differs vastly from that of most Indonesian Muslims, with the exception of the Islamist communities of Aceh, the northernmost province of Sumatra. The Islamic beliefs of most Indonesian Muslims are basically syncretic, and a literal interpretation of the Qur'an is still restricted to a minority of believers.

JI's goal is to create a caliphate, ruled by Islamic law, in the entire region spanning from Myanmar in the west to the Philippines in the east. The group's members hope this Islamic state will in time become part of the larger caliphate that al-Qaeda envisions as governing the worldwide Muslim community.

JI operatives have established personal and operational ties with top al-Qaeda leaders, including bin Laden, and have attacked similar kinds of civilian targets. Thus far, the most devastating of those attacks has been the October 2002 bombings that hit two nightclubs almost simultaneously in Bali. Most of the nearly 202 people who were killed were Australian and

Police escort a Thai man accused of plotting a series of attacks in Thailand to a court hearing in Bangkok. Authorities believe the man was a member of the Asian terrorist organization Jemaah Islamiyah, which hopes one day to unify much of Southeast Asia under Islamic law.

Western vacationers, but local Buddhists, who represent the majority group in Bali, were also among the victims.

Money, Government Complicity, and Religious Justifications

Training fighters, acquiring weapons, and providing logistical support for terrorist operations requires money. Some Islamist terrorist organizations have found a ready source of funds through the misappropriation of charitable donations. ***Zakat***, the requirement that Muslims donate a portion of their income to charity, is one of the so-called Five Pillars of Islam, the basic obligations of the faith. In some cases, unfortunately, organizations set up to collect and distribute *zakat* donations—such as al-Haramain Islamic Foundation—have been accused of funneling money to Islamist terrorists. Occasionally, Islamist terrorist organizations receive help from governments (many, though not all, of these groups operate legally and in the open, through an affiliated non-governmental organization or political party). Sometimes, for political or strategic reasons, Muslim governments support Islamists in neighboring states. For example, Kashmiri separatists have long received assistance and encouragement from a succession of Pakistani governments, both democratic and military, as did the Taliban in Afghanistan before its fall in late 2001. In other cases, the financial help comes from more distant sources—such as the governments and citizens of Saudi Arabia and other Gulf states (United Arab Emirates, Kuwait, Qatar, Bahrain), or even Shiite Iran. Some Islamist groups fund their terrorist attacks through a variety of criminal activities, including kidnapping for ransom, drug smuggling, theft, bank robbery, and credit card fraud—methods also used by European radical Muslims to finance their own terrorist operations.

Unlike the publicity-conscious Osama bin Laden, some Islamist leaders try to remain anonymous in their roles as heads of terrorist organizations.

This sign marks the headquarters of al-Haramain Islamic Foundation in Bangladesh. Although the foundation has been banned by the United States, Saudi Arabia, and other countries because it has distributed charitable donations to terrorist organizations, it continues to operate openly in some parts of Asia.

Such, according to experts, was the case with Abu Bakar Ba'asyir, the alleged leader of Jemaah Islamiyah in Southeast Asia. Though he frequently preached jihad, there is scant evidence that Ba'asyir personally committed violent acts. Of course, from a moral—and, in many countries, a legal—standpoint, there is little distinction between the person who recruits and encourages a murderer and the person who actually does the killing. The role in Islamic terrorism of self-described "spiritual leaders" who preach jihad is especially significant because, as a rule, Islamists do not engage in terrorism unless some credible religious figure gives his blessing to that method. Thus the inflammatory words of an imam in, say, the United Kingdom might foment and legitimize deadly violence in Indonesia or Algeria.

Targets and "Collateral Damage"

Islamist terrorists' targets are usually, but not always, Westerners. Americans and Israelis are often prime targets. The Christians of some regions are always marked. In Indonesia's Maluku and Sulawesi islands, for example, the Soldiers of Jihad focus on murdering Christians, who are also permanent targets of terrorism in Pakistan. Other targets may include political and cultural figures who criticize or oppose Islamists, such as Pakistan's president, Pervez Musharraf—the target of at least two assassination attempts by Islamists in 2004 alone.

As with terrorists motivated by other ideologies, Islamic terrorists often directly target civilians. The killing of noncombatants—something that is prohibited by the Qur'an—is frequently justified by claims that these people are complicit in their government's repression of Muslims or its "war against Islam." (And at the ideological extreme, Wahhabism has traditionally condoned—according to some, even required—the killing of infidels.) Because of the indiscriminate nature of much terrorism and the significant Muslim populations in some societies in which it is carried out, Muslims are frequently among the casualties. In such cases, Islamist terrorists often identify these victims as involuntary "martyrs" who will go to heaven. But Islamic terrorists may also target members of rival Muslim sects. This is the case particularly in Pakistan, where the Sunni Lashkar-e-Jhangvi (Army of Jhangvi), named after an assassinated leader, targets Shia Muslims as well as Christians.

Muslim activist members of the Jammu and Kashmir Liberation Forum demonstrate in Srinagar, India. The province of Kashmir, which is predominantly Muslim, became part of India when the British colony was partitioned in 1947. Since then, Pakistan and India have gone to war several times over the territory, which has also become a center of ongoing terrorist activity.

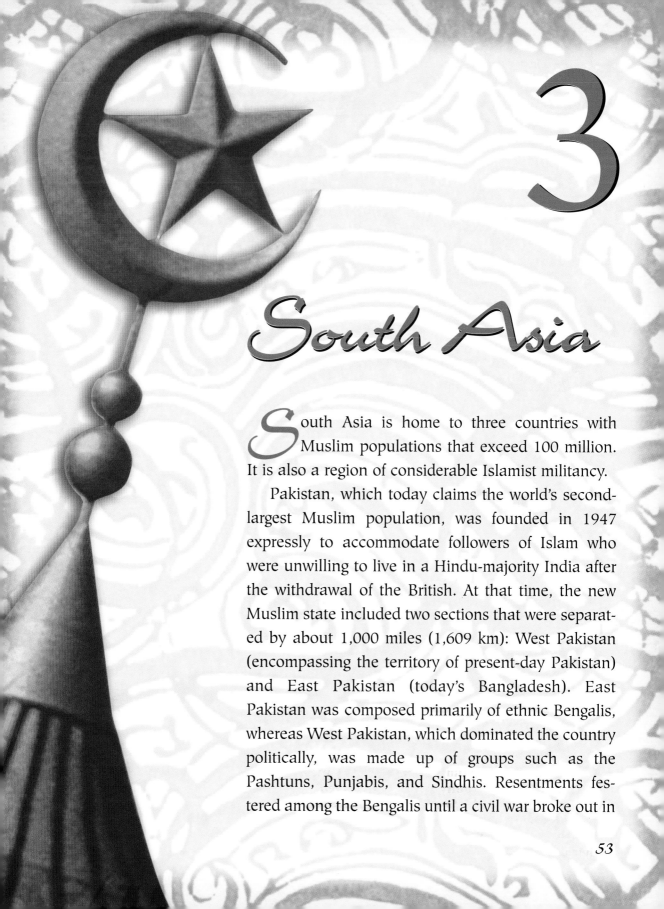

3

South Asia

South Asia is home to three countries with Muslim populations that exceed 100 million. It is also a region of considerable Islamist militancy.

Pakistan, which today claims the world's second-largest Muslim population, was founded in 1947 expressly to accommodate followers of Islam who were unwilling to live in a Hindu-majority India after the withdrawal of the British. At that time, the new Muslim state included two sections that were separated by about 1,000 miles (1,609 km): West Pakistan (encompassing the territory of present-day Pakistan) and East Pakistan (today's Bangladesh). East Pakistan was composed primarily of ethnic Bengalis, whereas West Pakistan, which dominated the country politically, was made up of groups such as the Pashtuns, Punjabis, and Sindhis. Resentments festered among the Bengalis until a civil war broke out in

1971 and, with help from India, East Pakistan won its independence, becoming the People's Republic of Bangladesh. Today Islamic fundamentalism flourishes in Pakistan and appears to be growing in Bangladesh.

India remains overwhelmingly Hindu. But because it is so populous—the country has more than a billion inhabitants—its 12 percent Muslim minority constitutes the world's third-largest Muslim population. And India has seen a measure of Islamist-based violence, principally over the issue of the Muslim-majority state of Jammu and Kashmir.

Bangladesh

The militant Islamist groups of Bangladesh are a potentially important political force for several reasons. First, they have ties to the powerful military—which over the course of Bangladesh's brief history has repeatedly intervened in the running of the government. In addition, Bangladesh suffers from extreme poverty, widespread official corruption, and weak rule of law. Under these circumstances, militant Islamic groups may hold considerable attraction. Some analysts fear that Bangladesh, with the fourth-largest Muslim population in the world, is being drawn into the whirlpool of Islamist radicalism.

The local Islamist group, Jamaat-e-Islami, has joined the political process. In 2001 the group gained 17 of the 300 seats in Bangladesh's Parliament and became part of the ruling coalition of the Bangladesh Nationalist Party. Jamaat-e-Islami's leader, Motiur Rahman Nizami, and his colleague Ali Ahsan are members of the cabinet. The party's youth wing, Islami Chhatra Shibir, is part of an international structure of Islamist youth groups, which includes the International Islamic Federation of Student Organizations and the World Assembly of Muslim Youth. The youth group leaders, trained in Deobandi madrassas, are influential at Chittagong University, located in the major Bangladesh city of the same name. Youth members have been involved in the assassinations of secular party

Supporters of Jamaat-e-Islami shout anti-Israel and anti-U.S. slogans during a demonstration in Dhaka, Bangladesh.

activists, such as Gopal Krishna Muhuri, a leading secular humanist and principal of Chittagong's Nazirhat College.

But Jamaat-e-Islami is not the only radical Islamist group in Bangladesh. Harkat-ul-Jihad-al-Islami (the Party of Islamic Jihad), led by Shawkat Osman (also known by his alias, Sheikh Farid), has strong and well-known ties to Osama bin Laden. The organization, formed in 1992, was one of the groups that forced author Taslima Nasrin, a critic of Islam's treatment of women, into exile by putting a price on her head in 1993. Fazlul Rahman, leader of the Jihad Movement in Bangladesh, was one of the original signatories of Osama bin Laden's jihad declaration against the West, issued on February 23, 1998.

India

India is the world's second most populous country, behind only China, and in the coming decades, demographers expect its population to surpass

An Indian policeman frisks a Kashmiri voter outside a polling booth during municipal elections in Anantnag, India. Security is always tight in Kashmir because of the threat of violence by Muslims who wish to force a referendum on the province's status.

that of its Asian neighbor. India's Muslim population currently exceeds 125 million—which is slightly more than that of Egypt (the largest Arab country), Saudi Arabia, and Morocco combined. Nonetheless, Muslims make up only about 12 percent of India's billion-plus population, and they constitute a majority in just one of the country's states: Jammu and Kashmir, in northernmost India. A large concentration of Muslims also lives in the western state of Gujarat, which borders Pakistan.

India is a democracy—in fact, it is the world's largest democracy. But its Hindu majority has increasingly adopted a hard line toward the Muslim minority, which, feeling increasingly threatened, is itself becoming more radicalized. Tensions have flared in many areas, but nowhere is the situation more volatile than in Jammu and Kashmir. There Muslim separatists have waged a bloody and long-running insurgency. In this fight they have received support from Pakistan as well as Islamist radicals from around the world, and since the early 1990s the largest Kashmiri separatist group, Hizbul Mujahideen, has been joined by Arab militants.

The troubles in Kashmir go back to the founding of Pakistan. In 1947, the year Pakistan and India gained their independence, the strongly Muslim region of Kashmir was divided between the countries, with a largely uninhabited part going to China. India retained the most populous and largest region. Kashmir, which is claimed in its entirety by Pakistan, has been the cause, either directly or indirectly, of three wars between India and Pakistan. Tensions remain high as the result of repeated crises and ongoing Islamist terrorism. Should the Kashmir issue ignite another war between India and Pakistan, the results could be catastrophic, as both countries now have nuclear weapons.

Pakistan

Founded specifically for the Indian subcontinent's Muslims, Pakistan remains an overwhelmingly Muslim country (according to a recent estimate,

Muttahida Majlis-e-Amal, an alliance of six Islamist parties, has become a strong political force in Pakistan. The poster gives a good indication of where the alliance's sympathies lie.

97 percent of Pakistanis follow Islam). But the Muslim population is divided between a Sunni majority and a substantial Shiite minority. More important, however, considerable tensions exist between those who favor a more secular society and government and Islamic fundamentalists who want Pakistan to follow the Sharia. Pakistan has been a major source of Islamist terrorism.

Pakistan ("Land of the Pure" in Urdu, the country's main language) lost a substantial amount of territory in the 1971 war that led to the creation of Bangladesh, but it nonetheless retains certain advantages over most other Muslim states. Under British rule, it developed a large and competent educated class. And Pakistani scientists were able to set up a successful nuclear-weapons program; the country detonated its first test bomb in 1998, becoming the only Muslim-majority country in the nuclear "club."

Pakistan's Deobandi school of thought is one of the three major wellsprings of Islamist terrorism today. (The other two are Egypt's Muslim Brotherhood and the Saudi Wahhabis.) Islamist terrorism in Pakistan has expanded in two directions. First, terrorists have targeted the Pakistani government, which they regard as insufficiently Islamic. At least four attempts have been made on the life of President Pervez Musharraf, a general who came to power as the result of a 1999 military coup. Musharraf particularly angered Islamist militants by cooperating with the United States in its "war on terrorism." Suicide bombers have also unsuccessfully targeted Pakistani prime ministers. A 2004 attempt on the life of Shaukat Aziz, an influential finance minister whom Musharraf promoted to the post of prime minister, left at least nine people dead. Second, Pakistani-based Islamic terrorism has targeted India, especially over the Kashmir issue. Islamic fundamentalists want to separate Muslim-majority Kashmir from India (and, as noted previously, the Pakistani government has sponsored their efforts).

Major Terrorist Groups of South Asia

Jamiat-ul-Ansar (formerly Harakat ul Mujahideen, "Islamic Freedom Fighters' Group") was established in Kashmir in the mid-1980s. Led by Farooq Kashmiri Khalil, an al-Qaeda supporter, the group shifted to Afghanistan after the fall of the Taliban in 2001. It has several thousand armed supporters, and the capability of

Police display hooded and handcuffed members of the banned group Lashkar-e-Jhangvi, along with their confiscated weapons, at a police station in Lahore, Pakistan.

recruiting many more through its network of madrassas. Its members have staged operations in Myanmar, Tajikistan, and Bosnia.

The Pakistani group **Khudam-ul Islam** (formerly Jaish-e-Muhammad, or "Army of Muhammad") was established in 2000 by Maulana Masood Azhar, a cleric personally connected to Osama bin Laden. It built up its membership by incorporating former Jamiat-ul-Ansar members.

Lashkar-e-Tayyiba (Army of the Righteous), active since 1993 and based in Pakistan, is the military wing of Markaz-ud-Dawa-wal-Irshad, a political party whose declared mission is the spreading of fundamentalist Islam through missionary, or "*dawa*," activities. In 2004 Lashkar-e-Tayyiba participated in attacks against U.S. forces in Iraq.

Jamaat-ud Dawa (Society of the Call) is closely related to—and, analysts suggest, may simply be a renamed version of—Lashkar-e-Tayyiba, which was outlawed by the Pakistani government in 2002. Its leaders, Hafiz Saeed and Tahir Rabbani, have international ambitions and close links to al-Qaeda.

Lashkar-e-Jhangvi (Army of Jhangvi), the armed wing of Sipah-e-Sahaba, is a Sunni Muslim group in Pakistan that collaborates with al-Qaeda. It has traditionally targeted Shiites.

It should be noted that terrorist groups often change their names. This tactic is intended to confuse the authorities, not only making counterterrorism more difficult but also enabling terrorist groups to circumvent legal bans that governments may put in place.

Muslim cleric Abu Bakar Ba'asyir is surrounded by police officers outside a court in Jakarta, December 2004. Authorities suspect that Ba'asyir is the head of Jemaah Islamiyah, although in September 2003 an Indonesian court acquitted him of terrorism charges. He was rearrested in 2004 and charged with involvement in a series of deadly bombings in Indonesia between 2002 and 2004.

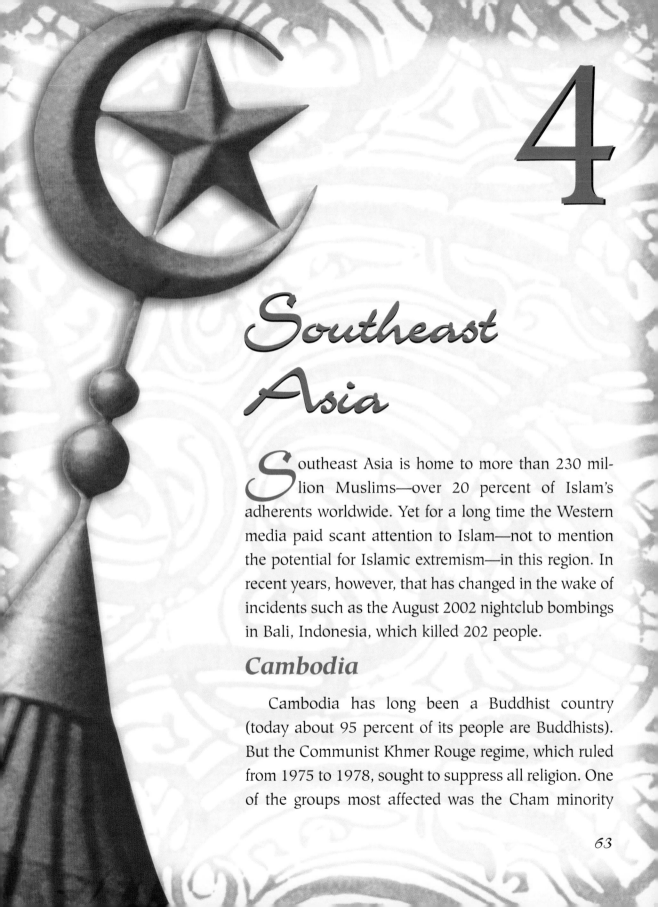

4

Southeast Asia

Southeast Asia is home to more than 230 million Muslims—over 20 percent of Islam's adherents worldwide. Yet for a long time the Western media paid scant attention to Islam—not to mention the potential for Islamic extremism—in this region. In recent years, however, that has changed in the wake of incidents such as the August 2002 nightclub bombings in Bali, Indonesia, which killed 202 people.

Cambodia

Cambodia has long been a Buddhist country (today about 95 percent of its people are Buddhists). But the Communist Khmer Rouge regime, which ruled from 1975 to 1978, sought to suppress all religion. One of the groups most affected was the Cham minority (often referred to as "Khmer Islam"), Sunni Muslims also present in neighboring Vietnam. The Khmer Rouge leaders killed most Cham people, especially the religious leaders; mosques were destroyed or desecrated; and Muslims were not allowed to worship.

Historically, the Cham have practiced a form of Islam noted for its syncretic elements. The Cham clergy, like their Buddhist counterparts, shave their heads and faces. They also dress completely in white and believe in the power of magic and sorcery. After their near destruction during the Khmer Rouge period, many impoverished Cham communities have come under the influence of Saudi-financed Wahhabi preachers. While the Cham and the radical Islamists in their midst still constitute a very small minority, the flow of money in support of a radical Islamist ideology is a trend that bears watching.

Cham Muslims who fled persecution in Cambodia worship in a mosque in Vientiane, Laos.

Indonesia

More than 200 million Indonesians follow Islam, giving Indonesia the largest Muslim population in the world. It is also the main focus of Islamist terrorism in Southeast Asia and one of the most important centers for terrorism on the planet. Geography constitutes a major advantage for the terrorists: the country consists of more than 13,000 islands, and it is all but impossible for the government to control the entirety of its far-flung territory.

Islam was introduced to Indonesia not through military conquest, as happened in most other Muslim-majority countries, but through missionary activities that followed traditional trade routes across the Indian Ocean. Largely for this reason, many aspects of other religions were included in Indonesian Islamic practice. Some islands, especially Bali and Irian Jaya, did not even convert to Islam, and some, like the Maluku and Sulawesi islands, were Christianized by Dutch colonizers. Still others, especially Sumatra (the Indonesian island closest to the Middle East), adopted a much stricter form of Islam.

Islamist terrorism in Indonesia is largely represented by Jemaah Islamiyah (Islamic Society), or JI. The organization, which has long-standing ties with al-Qaeda, is also active in neighboring countries, especially Malaysia, the Philippines, and Singapore, as well as the more distant Thailand and Cambodia. Other militant organizations in Indonesia include the Front Pembela Islam (Islamic Defenders Front) and Laskar Jundullah. The Front Pembela Islam was formed in 1998 and is led by Saudi-educated Habib Muhammad Rizieq Shihab. Many of its leaders are at least part Arab. Laskar Jundullah, the military wing of the Indonesian Mujahideen Council, belongs to the Committee for the Establishment of Shariah Law in Indonesia and may have connections with JI.

International outrage over terrorist attacks targeting Westerners in Indonesia forced the country's government to take stronger measures to stop Islamist militants. This picture shows a well-equipped group of Indonesian anti-terror police.

Malaysia

To a very large extent, Malaysia is a colonial British creation. It was formed from relatively autonomous Muslim polities (including the sultanates of Kelantan and Negri Sembilan). Many of its constituent states are still technically ruled by dynasties. Although Islam is the official state religion, only about 6 in 10 Malaysians are Muslim, according to the government's 2000 census figures.

Malaysia has been less affected by militant Islamism than other countries with Muslim majorities. But that is not to say the country is immune from Islamist extremist groups. The country's foremost terrorist organization, Kumpulan Mujahideen Malaysia (KMM), is believed to have ties with JI. Established in 1995 by an Afghani named Zainon Ismail, KMM is also suspected of coordinating with a radical group based in Indonesia known as Mujahideen Kompak.

A small number of Thai Islamic secessionists are believed to have found safe haven in the Malaysian sultanates close to the Thailand border. Some analysts expect this trend to grow in coming years.

The Philippines

Spain colonized the Philippines in the 16th century, but the Spanish managed to exercise complete control only on Luzon and the other large islands. The United States took possession of the Philippines after defeating Spain in the Spanish-American War of 1898. The islands gained commonwealth status in 1935 and became fully independent in 1946, following World War II.

The Philippines is Asia's only Roman Catholic–majority state. Most Filipinos have Spanish names, speak English as a second language to their native Tagalog, and are practicing Catholics. However, Muslims constitute a large minority on the second-largest island, Mindanao, and its neighboring islands. Alienation is a common experience among this group. Secessionist Muslim movements have been active since the 1980s, first under the leadership of the Moro Liberation Front and now under the Moro Islamic Liberation Front (MILF). (A Spanish term originally used to denote a member of the Arab-Berber Muslim people who conquered Spain in the eighth century, *Moro*, or "Moor," is now used to signify any Filipino Muslim.) The main goal of the Filipino Moros is to separate the Muslim majority islands from the Philippines. While many Muslim activists in the

Members of the Moro Islamic Liberation Front (MILF) show off their weapons in the Maguindanao province, southern Philippines. The MILF has been fighting to form a Muslim state separate from the predominantly Christian Philippines.

Philippines are not terrorists, there are at least two major Islamist terrorist organizations in the country, Abu Sayyaf (named after the sword of an early Islamic militant), and the local branch of JI. Both of the groups occasionally cooperate with the MILF.

Abu Sayyaf has long-standing ties with al-Qaeda. Its founder, the late Abdurajak Janjalani (killed in a shoot-out with security forces in 1998), was a veteran of al-Qaeda's terrorist training camps in Afghanistan. Abu Sayyaf specializes in kidnapping foreigners for ransom, and it is especially active on the island of Basilan. Its membership is estimated at a few hundred at most.

Singapore

The small and prosperous island-nation of Singapore is located south of the Malay Peninsula and east of the Indonesian island of Sumatra. Its population of about 4.3 million is multiethnic (with a Chinese majority and significant Malay and Indian minorities) and multireligious (including Buddhists, Muslims, Christians, Taoists, and Sikhs).

Singapore is noted for its tight social control. The government makes use of a formidable internal-security apparatus and laws that, for example, allow the detention of suspects for up to two years without trial. This has certainly mitigated the risk of terrorist attacks within Singapore's borders.

Nevertheless, Islamist terrorists from other countries in the region have used Singapore as a base; the island offers easy access to nearby areas of Muslim extremist activity (including Indonesia, Malaysia, and the Philippines). In addition, as a hub of business and commercial activity, Singapore itself has a wealth of potential targets for terrorist attacks. Its maritime commercial lines, essential to Singapore's economy, are believed to be particularly vulnerable.

In 2001 Singapore authorities rolled up a Jemaah Islamiyah cell that had been surveying potential targets since 1997. Most of the 15 JI members

continued on p. 72

Anatomy of a Terrorist Attack

On September 9, 2004, a suicide bomber detonated a massive car bomb outside the Australian embassy in Jakarta, Indonesia. The blast killed 9 people and injured more than 180.

Jemaah Islamiyah quickly claimed responsibility for the attack. "We decided to settle accounts with Australia," its statement on an Islamic website said, "one of the worst enemies of God and Islam . . . and a mujahedeen brother succeeded in carrying out a martyr operation with a car bomb against the Australian embassy." However, no Australians were actually killed in the attack; the dead were all Indonesians. Most of the injured were Indonesians as well, though a few Australian embassy workers sustained minor injuries. The fact that the majority of the victims were most likely Muslims did not appear to be of concern to JI; as with Osama bin Laden and al-Qaeda, JI implies that devout Muslims who die in their jihad are guaranteed a place in Paradise, and those who might have been cooperating with the "infidels" deserve to die.

Indonesian and Australian authorities soon identified two Malaysians as the main suspects in the embassy bombing: Azahari bin Husin and Noordin Mohamed Top. Both were also involved in the 2002 Bali nightclub bombings (which killed 202 people) and in the 2003 bombing of the Marriott Hotel in Jakarta (which killed 12). Before moving to Indonesia in 2001, both men received training in al-Qaeda camps in Afghanistan and then trained alongside Abu Sayyaf and al-Qaeda militants in parts of the Philippine island of Mindanao controlled by the insurgent separatists of the Moro Islamic Liberation Front.

Australia's flag flies in front of the severely damaged building that held its embassy in Jakarta.

(continued on next page)

Medical professionals help an Indonesian victim of the September 2004 suicide bombing.

Azahari, an engineer by training, is JI's chief bomb maker. In the 1980s he obtained a doctorate at the University of Reading in England. During the same

involved were Singapore residents, and 8 had spent time in al-Qaeda training camps.

In October 2001, JI members assisted two al-Qaeda operatives as they videotaped potential targets in Singapore, including visiting U.S. Navy vessels and personnel; U.S. aircraft and facilities; the embassies of the United States, Israel, the United Kingdom, and Australia; the Singapore Ministry decade he apparently became an Islamist after meeting JI's "spiritual leader" and founder, Abu Bakar Ba'ashyir. Azahari was living in Malaysia, where he held a position as a university lecturer and had a wife and two children, before disappearing in 2001.

Noordin is a graduate of the Malaysian Technical Institute, but his specialty is as a terrorist financier and recruiter of suicide bombers. He has extensive ties with al-Qaeda and is thought to have received funds from that organization.

The fact that Noordin and Azahari lived in Indonesia for three years and managed to elude detection by the authorities, despite their involvement in two major terrorist incidents before the embassy bombing, suggests that an extensive network was in place to support them. Although Indonesian authorities arrested several people in the weeks after the 2004 attack, Noordin and Azahari slipped away and were still at large as of February 2005. The embassy bombing also provides a glimpse of the regional, rather than simply national, nature of Islamic terrorism in Asia. The leading suspects were citizens of one Asian country (Malaysia), received training in another (the Philippines), and carried out their attacks in a third (Indonesia).

of Defense complex; and office buildings housing U.S. firms. U.S. authorities caught wind of the danger when the videotape of the surveillance mission was found in the rubble of an al-Qaeda house in Afghanistan. In early December 2001, they alerted Singapore of the cell members' activities.

Between December 9 and 24, Singapore authorities made the arrests. By that point, the JI members had already stored 3.9 tons of ammonium nitrate, commonly used in large vehicle bombs, and were looking to acquire another 16.7 tons.

Thailand

Thailand is one of the few Asian countries that has never known European colonial rule. As Siam, it ruled over non-Thai areas in what are today Cambodia and Malaysia. The Thais are largely of southern Chinese origin and are overwhelmingly Buddhist. But the country's four southern-most provinces—Pattani, Yala, Narathiwat, and Satun—which were annexed by the Siamese kingdom in the 19th century, are ethnically Malay and Muslim. Islamist activities are largely limited to these

Cambodian policemen escort two Thai men accused of being members of Jemaah Islamiyah to a court in Phnom Penh.

provinces, a region conquered but never assimilated by Siam's Buddhist regimes.

Until recently Thailand's "southern problem" was an ethnic one (though the government in Bangkok steadfastly denied the existence of any problem at all). However, it was discovered that JI had first developed the plans for the 2002 Bali bombings during meetings in Thailand earlier that year. And in 2003 JI planned attacks on Western embassies and tourist sites in Thailand, although these were uncovered and prevented.

Two Afghan men executed by the Taliban government. From 1996 until 2001, the Taliban ruled Afghanistan under an extremely strict interpretation of Islamic law, or Sharia. Harsh punishments were meted out for a host of transgressions.

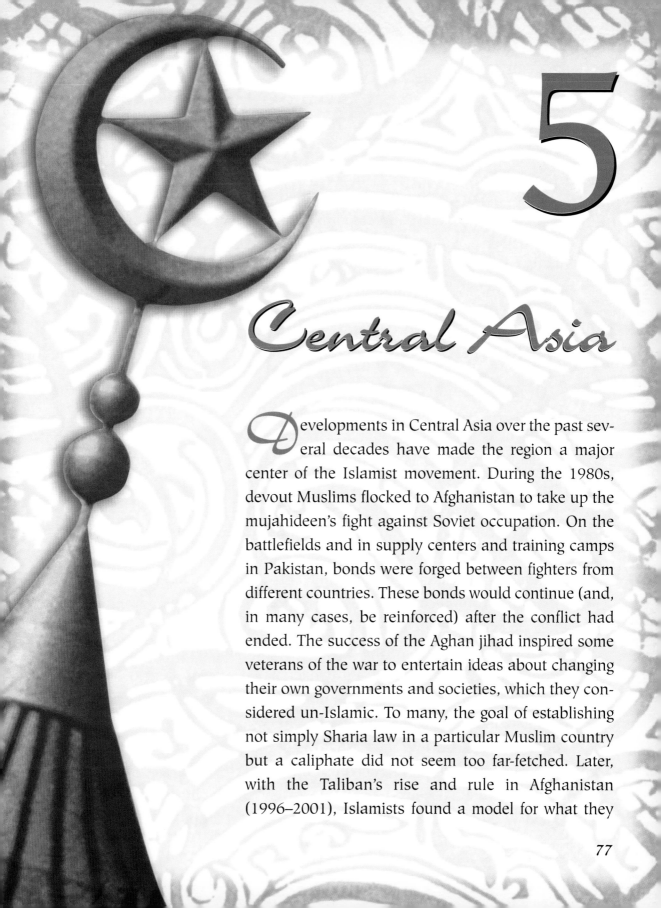

5

Central Asia

$\mathcal{D}$evelopments in Central Asia over the past several decades have made the region a major center of the Islamist movement. During the 1980s, devout Muslims flocked to Afghanistan to take up the mujahideen's fight against Soviet occupation. On the battlefields and in supply centers and training camps in Pakistan, bonds were forged between fighters from different countries. These bonds would continue (and, in many cases, be reinforced) after the conflict had ended. The success of the Aghan jihad inspired some veterans of the war to entertain ideas about changing their own governments and societies, which they considered un-Islamic. To many, the goal of establishing not simply Sharia law in a particular Muslim country but a caliphate did not seem too far-fetched. Later, with the Taliban's rise and rule in Afghanistan (1996–2001), Islamists found a model for what they regarded as appropriate Islamic governance, as well as refuge and training camps for terrorists.

Meanwhile, in 1991, the Soviet Union had collapsed and its former Central Asian republics had gained independence. The Soviet Communists had long suppressed religion, and the removal of Soviet control created space for a renaissance in Islamic faith and practice in traditionally Muslim Central Asia. Islamic fundamentalism soon appeared, and in Central Asian countries such as Uzbekistan, draconian measures to control Islam have only increased the appeal of militant Islam.

Afghanistan

Before the fall of the ruling Taliban in 2001, Afghanistan was the primary center of international Islamist terrorism. Today its global role is practically gone, but the country remains a powerful ideological symbol—the place where al-Qaeda formed, trained operatives, and established its hierarchy.

Afghanistan is the meeting place of Iranian, Turkic, and Pakistani cultures. The country became the focus of worldwide Islamist activity following the Soviet invasion in 1979. Under the supervision of al-Qaeda, tens of thousands of foreign Islamist militants set up operations during the 1990s and continued to be based and trained in well-organized camps until the end of 2001.

Virtually all of Afghanistan's population is Muslim (about 80 percent Sunni and 19 percent Shia). But while shared religion helped unify the resistance against the Soviets, ethnicity rather than religion became the dominant factor in Afghan politics after the Soviet withdrawal in 1989. The country descended into lawlessness and chaos as ethnically based factions and warlords from Afghanistan's four largest ethnic groups—the Pashtuns, Tajiks, Uzbeks, and Hazara—competed with one another for regional power or fought for control of the capital, Kabul.

After the Soviet Union withdrew from Afghanistan in 1989, the Afghan mujahideen—who had united to battle the Red Army—splintered into factions and fought one another for power. This paved the way for the rise of the Taliban. Pictured here are members of the Taliban during a 1996 battle with the Northern Alliance near Kabul.

The factional fighting claimed thousands of lives and brought more destruction to a country that had already been ravaged by the decade-long Soviet occupation; Kabul, which had remained largely untouched during the struggle against the Soviets, was destroyed in this new round of fighting. Not surprisingly, weary Afghans initially welcomed the Taliban, which promised a return to order. A Pashtun-dominated group that was created in the early 1990s by Pakistan's intelligence service and Pakistani Islamists, the Taliban was composed mainly of former Afghan refugees who had studied in madrassas in Pakistan during the 1980s. In late 1994 Taliban forces took the Afghan city of Kandahar, and from there they expanded their control; by September 1996 the Taliban had conquered Kabul and most of the country, becoming the de facto government of

Afghanistan (albeit one recognized only by Pakistan, Saudi Arabia, and the United Arab Emirates).

The Taliban regime imposed an extreme interpretation of Sharia. Public interactions between members of the opposite sex were all but eliminated, and the rights of women were severely restricted. Women were not permitted to receive an education, practice a profession, or go outside the home unless accompanied by a male relative and covered from head to toe by a burka. Men were required to wear a beard. Almost all forms of entertainment, from movies and music to kite flying, were banned. Statues and other works of art from Afghanistan's rich cultural past—most famously, a pair of centuries-old Buddhas carved into a mountainside in Bamiyan—were destroyed. The penalties for crimes or transgressions against the Taliban's version of Sharia law were severe, ranging from public beatings to amputation of limbs to beheading.

During the rule of the Taliban, women were not permitted to appear in public unless wearing a burka.

The Taliban, led by a semi-literate former madrassa student named Mullah Muhammad Omar, also sought to export its version of Islam by helping Islamist terrorist groups from throughout the region. These included the Islamic Movement of Uzbekistan, Kashmiri separatist groups, China's East Turkestan Islamic Movement, Jemaah Islamiyah, and al-Qaeda. Osama bin Laden, who by this point was already settled in Afghanistan, formed a close relationship with the Taliban shortly after it gained power. It was during this time that al-Qaeda received protection from the Taliban and began planning the attacks of September 11, 2001. Because the Taliban supported al-Qaeda, the United States intervened to remove it in late 2001.

Despite its defeat at the hands of the U.S.-led coalition, the establishment of an interim Afghan government, and the free elections that made Hamid Karzai Afghanistan's president, as of early 2005 the Taliban continued to operate, albeit increasingly on the margins, from its base in Pakistan's mountains along the Afghanistan border. In addition, new Islamist radical groups such as Jaïsh-e-Muslim (Army of Muslims) had appeared or reappeared in Afghanistan. All were dominated by the ethnic Pashtuns, who also make up a large majority in the North-West Frontier province of Pakistan. These radicals seemed to show just as much interest in establishing or reestablishing Pashtun supremacy in Afghan politics as in pushing for an Islamic caliphate, starting with Afghanistan.

China

In a cultural sense, China bears little resemblance to the world's Islamic countries. Nearly 92 percent of its people are members of the Han ethnic group, which has dominated Chinese civilization for millennia. However, China is home to almost 20 million Muslims. Although this constitutes a small percentage in an overall population of approximately 1.3 billion— and although the majority of China's Muslims are largely assimilated into

Chinese Muslims study Arabic in a school in the western Xinjiang region. In recent years the Chinese government has justified a crackdown on Muslims in Xinjiang by linking militant Uygurs there to terrorism. However, in the view of many observers, the Uygurs are driven more by nationalism than by Islamist ideology.

the dominant Han culture—there are more than 7.5 million Muslim Uygurs in China's northwestern Xinjiang region, which is also known as Chinese Turkestan. Because members of China's Turkic-speaking Uygur minority have in recent years perpetrated acts of terrorism in pursuit of independence from China—and some, presumably, seek the creation of a Central Asian Islamic caliphate—China is often included in overviews of Asian Islamism.

China's Communist government has been particularly alarmed by recent developments in Xinjiang for several reasons. Not least among Beijing's worries is the proximity of Xinjiang to the volatile Central Asian states of the former Soviet Union. Islamism has sprung up in those Muslim-majority countries since the fall of the Soviet Union. Moreover, Uygur minorities also live in Kazakhstan, Tajikistan, and Kyrgyzstan, and China's Uygurs—who have resisted assimilation into Chinese culture—have greater affinities with their Turkic cousins to the west than their Han fellow citizens of China. While religion plays a comparatively minor role in Chinese society as a whole (and the government prohibits the practice of organized religion outside of state-sanctioned mosques, temples, and churches), Islam is central to the political, social, economic, and personal life of the Uygurs. Then there is the East Turkestan Islamic Movement, a Xinjiang separatist group that China says is a terrorist organization.

The Chinese authorities blame Muslim Uygurs for more than 200 violent incidents between 1990 and 2001—a claim disputed by international human rights groups. Particularly since the September 11, 2001, attacks on the United States, the Chinese government has attempted to define violence in Xinjiang within the context of international Islamic terrorism, although some observers believe the Uygur cause has more to do with nationalism. In any event, in the period 2001–2002, the Chinese government claimed it arrested more than 100 Chinese terrorists who were trained in Afghan camps, and in September 2002, following the capture of 21 Uygur terrorists in Afghanistan, the United Nations added the East Turkestan Islamic Movement to its "list of terrorists and terrorist supporters associated with Osama bin Laden and his al-Qaeda network."

Beijing has employed a variety of methods to solve its "Muslim problem." It has promoted ethnic Han immigration to Xinjiang while aggressively "encouraging" Uygurs to leave the region. As a result of these internal colonization and emigration policies, Uygurs now constitute a minority in Xinjiang. The government has also responded harshly to Uygur dissidents, most famously in 1997, when police fired into a crowd of students demonstrating for an independent East Turkestan. About 30 protesters are believed to have been killed and nearly 200 wounded in the incident, which was followed by a series of Uygur demonstrations and terrorist attacks. These, in turn, provoked a severe government crackdown on Uygur dissidents—even, critics charge, those who had no involvement in anti-government violence.

Kazakhstan and Turkmenistan

Neither Kazakhstan nor Turkmenistan, which share a short border near the Caspian Sea, has been significantly affected by Islamism. Among the countries of Central Asia, Kazakhstan is the least Muslim; its population is almost equally divided between Muslims and Christians (mostly members of the Russian Orthodox Church). During the Soviet era, Moscow promoted large-scale immigration into Kazakhstan by ethnic Russians, and while many Russians departed after Kazakhstan gained independence, the large Russian/Slavic minority continues to play a significant role in the national culture. Kazakhstan has strong economic and military ties with Russia and, increasingly in recent years, with the West. Perhaps because of its largely Russian orientation, as well as its history of relatively cordial relations between Muslims and Russian Orthodox Christians, the strong Islamist influences that have arisen in much of Central Asia have yet to emerge in Kazakhstan.

Turkmenistan is a large country with a small population: in total area, it is bigger than California but has fewer than 5 million people. To the south, Turkmenistan borders two countries that have in recent years been centers of Islamic radicalism—Iran and Afghanistan. And about 9 in 10 citizens of Turkmenistan are Muslim (mostly Sunnis). Yet the country has not proved fertile ground for Islamists. Much of this might be attributable to the policies of President Saparmurat Niyazov, the self-styled Turkmenbashi ("father of the Turkmen"). A former Soviet Communist bureaucrat, Niyazov has muted Islamic influences, from within the country and from abroad, by creating a cult of personality around himself and by employing Soviet-style authoritarian measures. Interestingly, Niyazov has hinted that an unsuccessful coup attempt in late 2002 was the work of foreign powers that covet the country's rich resources, especially its abundant natural gas and oil deposits.

Kyrgyzstan

Like the authoritarian regimes of its neighbors China, Uzbekistan, Kazakhstan, and Tajikistan, the government of Kyrgyzstan has striven to suppress Islamist activities within its borders. Yet the country's rugged terrain, porous borders, and fairly weak military have enabled a variety of regional Islamist organizations to find safe haven in Kyrgyzstan. These include, or have included, the Islamic Movement of Uzbekistan as well as the Taliban and other Afghan Islamist groups.

Kyrgyzstan is led by Askar Akayev, a scientist who was appointed president in the waning days of the Soviet Union and has held on to power ever since. While Akayev's regime is arguably less repressive than those of other Central Asian countries, Kyrgyzstan's human rights record is spotty at best. A variety of sources, from Amnesty International and Human Rights Watch to the U.S. State Department, have detailed the regime's heavy-handed tactics for silencing dissent. Such tactics, critics contend, have included arresting political opponents for being affiliated with extremist groups such as the Islamic Movement of Uzbekistan, even when there appears to be no evidence to support that charge. While the government has legitimate concerns that Islamist extremism could spill over its borders, some observers suspect that the Akayev regime has used the threat of Islamism for political purposes.

Tajikistan

The majority of Tajikistan's population speaks Dari, a dialect of Farsi, rather than a Turkic tongue—a distinction that gives the people a more

Guards use sophisticated radiation detection devices to prevent the smuggling of nuclear materials at the border between Kazakhstan and Uzbekistan. During the Soviet era, nuclear weapons were tested and stored in Kazakhstan; experts fear that Asian terrorist groups may one day get their hands on the fuel to make a nuclear bomb.

Persian/Iranian identity and distinguishes them from the dominant Turkic peoples of Central Asia. Ethnic Tajiks make up the second-largest ethnic group in Afghanistan and are heavily concentrated in the country's mountainous northeastern regions, which are hard to control. Consequently, developments in Afghanistan have an immediate impact on Tajikistan. Since the 1979 Soviet invasion of Afghanistan, in which a number of Tajiks served as interpreters or soldiers, cross-border influences have increased dramatically. Well-armed Afghan Tajiks played a key role in Tajikistan's 1992–97 civil war.

In addition to Afghanistan, many Tajiks also live in Uzbekistan, and developments in that country have resonated in Tajikistan as well. In fact, Islamist activities in Tajikistan may be spurred less by local circumstances than by events and conditions in Uzbekistan and Afghanistan. Currently, the most active Islamist terrorist organization in Tajikistan is the Islamic Movement of Uzbekistan/Islamic Party of Turkestan.

Uzbekistan

Uzbekistan is both the most populous of the former Soviet republics of Central Asia and the only one to border all the others. (It borders Afghanistan as well.) Uzbekistan is also where the first—and still most important—Islamist organization in Central Asia, the Islamic Movement of Uzbekistan (IMU), was formed.

Uzbekistan's population is composed predominantly of Turkic-speaking ethnic Uzbeks. But the country is also home to a substantial minority of Farsi-speaking Tajiks, who have cultural and linguistic ties to Iran. Uzbekistan's Tajiks are concentrated in the important urban areas of Samarqand, Bukhara, Khiva, and Tashkent. Samarqand and Bukhara have been centers of high Islamic learning for centuries, at times competing with such better-known centers as Baghdad and Damascus. Tashkent, the capital of Uzbekistan, is by far the largest city in the entire region.

Uzbekistan has historically been a center of Islamic culture—and, more recently, of Islamist ideology, activity, and tensions. Its major cities—Samarqand, Bukhara, and Khiva—were the capitals of independent Muslim states known as khanates before Russia expanded its control into Central Asia. During the 1920s the Soviets encountered ferocious resistance in Uzbekistan when they tried to consolidate Communist control there.

The Islamic Movement of Uzbekistan, despite its name, does not confine its activities to Uzbekistan; rather, it is a regional terrorist organization.

As onlookers frown in disapproval, a young Uzbek Muslim tries to distribute religious literature—an activity prohibited by law in Uzbekistan—at a bus stop in Tashkent. Uzbekistan, like other Central Asian states, has imposed many restrictions on the practice of Islam. Some observers suspect that this has more to do with quashing political dissent than with addressing the threat of Islamist extremism—and that in the end the government's measures may only increase the appeal of militant Islam.

The IMU was founded in 1999 by a cleric named Takhir Yuldash and by Juma Namangani, a veteran of the Soviet army in Afghanistan. Upon returning from Afghanistan to the Fergana Valley—long a hotbed of Islamist activity—Namangani (whose *nom de guerre* was taken from his hometown, Namangan) studied with an Islamic scholar and embraced a radical Islamist outlook. After the collapse of the Soviet Union in 1991, he organized a group of Islamist vigilantes who punished robbers and other criminals. That group, which grew into a terrorist organization espousing the creation of a Central Asian caliphate, established ties with Kyrgyz, Tajik, and Uygur extremists. In June 2001, the IMU changed its name to the Islamic Party of Turkestan.

In late 2001 Namangani again fought in Afghanistan—this time in support of the Taliban. He is believed to have been killed in an American bombing raid. The group he cofounded, now exclusively under the leadership of Takhir Yuldash, is today based in Pakistan's tribal areas. It continues to be active in Kyrgyzstan, Tajikistan, Uzbekistan, Afghanistan, and Pakistan.

Indonesian Muslims protest outside the U.S. embassy in Jakarta. Indonesia was among a handful of Asian countries that tried to ignore the growing problem of Islamist extremism within its borders. That approach, experience has shown, is a recipe for disaster.

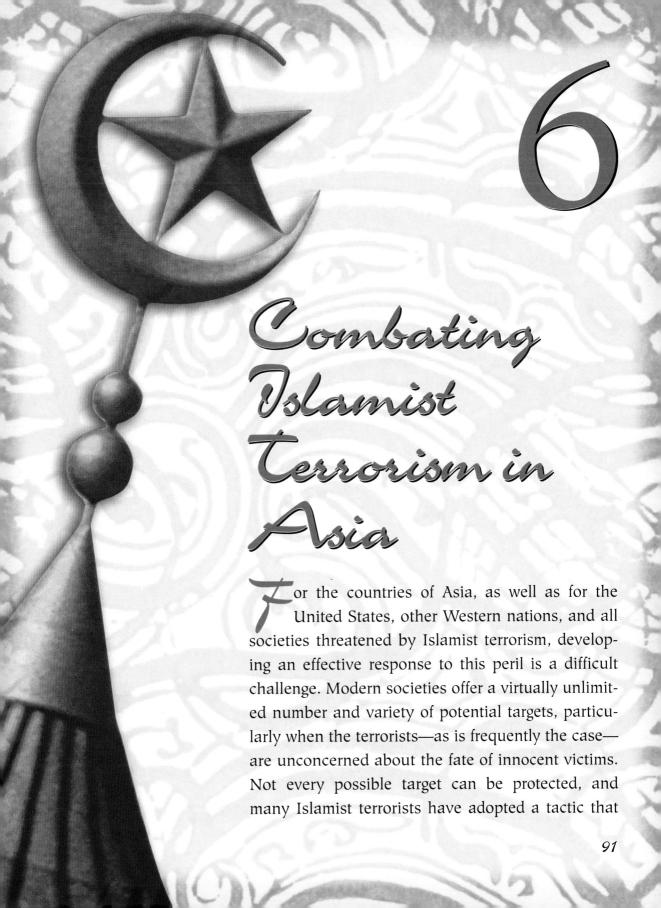

6

Combating Islamist Terrorism in Asia

For the countries of Asia, as well as for the United States, other Western nations, and all societies threatened by Islamist terrorism, developing an effective response to this peril is a difficult challenge. Modern societies offer a virtually unlimited number and variety of potential targets, particularly when the terrorists—as is frequently the case— are unconcerned about the fate of innocent victims. Not every possible target can be protected, and many Islamist terrorists have adopted a tactic that has confounded even the most security-conscious of societies, such as Israel: suicide bombing.

Mobility is a hallmark of the modern world. Within liberal democratic societies, freedom of movement is a deep-seated value. Even in countries that are somewhat more restrictive, participation in the global economy requires a certain degree of openness. And there are some countries that do not fully control their borders, or even all their territory (Asian countries such as Pakistan, Indonesia, and the Philippines are prominent examples). As a result, terrorists have been able to move with relative ease across national boundaries and to train and find refuge in remote areas (as well as in countries supportive of their goals).

Furthermore, while the goals of different Islamist terrorist organizations are not necessarily identical, many of these groups have found a great deal of common ground. They cooperate with one another in a variety of ways. And modern communications technologies facilitate coordination and control among different organizations, and between terrorist leaders and cells in different countries. The same Internet that lets people communicate with friends in faraway countries also enables computer-trained terrorists in Pakistan, Bali, or Mindanao to coordinate attacks in other countries.

All of the above merely hints at the challenges of combating Islamist terrorism. The problem is truly one of global proportions, and there are no easy solutions.

Counterterrorism in Asia

If no "magic bullet" exists by which nations might quickly and completely eliminate the threat of Islamist terrorism, experience has shown that some approaches are almost guaranteed not to work. Governments cannot ignore the existence of an Islamist problem in the hopes it will simply go away. Indonesia, for example, long denied that violent Islamism was growing on its soil. The country prided itself on its status as the

Indonesians surf the Internet at a shopping mall in Jakarta. The Internet has made it easier for radical groups to share plans and spread their ideologies.

world's largest Muslim democracy, as well as its tradition of religious tolerance. And acknowledgment of an Islamist problem would threaten Indonesia's tourist industry. After the Bali bombings of 2002, however, the problem could no longer be ignored—but by then it was too late for the roughly 200 victims who lost their lives to the Islamist terrorists. Similarly, analysts have suggested that the government of predominantly Buddhist Thailand—whose economy also relies heavily on tourism—is in denial over the extent of its incipient problem with Islamist extremism. In

Muslims burn an American flag during a protest rally. One of the goals of Islamist extremists in Asia (as well as other parts of the world) is to force the United States to withdraw militarily, economically, and culturally from Muslim lands—something that is not an option for U.S. policymakers.

December 2004, following deadly violence said to have been fomented by Islamist secessionists in Thailand's largely Muslim southern provinces, the government carpet-bombed those provinces—with an estimated 100 million origami paper birds, a symbol of peace.

If trying to placate Islamist extremists is unlikely to work, and if denying the existence of an Islamist problem almost guarantees that the problem will merely grow, the use of repressive measures also presents risks. Uzbekistan is a good case in point. In the name of combating Islamist terrorists (principally the IMU), the regime of Uzbekistan's longtime president, Islam Karimov, has restricted all forms of Muslim expression outside state-sanctioned mosques. By all accounts the government's tactics have been heavy-handed and frequently brutal. And this, many analysts believe, has not only alienated a large number of Uzbekistan's citizens, but also driven some otherwise moderate Uzbek Muslims into the fold of the extremists. Similarly, some analysts have suggested that China's ruthless crackdowns in the Xinjiang region have increased the appeal of militant Islam there. (Of course, the Chinese authorities have considerably more coercive power at their disposal than does the regime in Uzbekistan, and Islamism will never be a threat to the Chinese government as a whole, whereas it might be to the Karimov regime.)

In the countries of Asia with significant Muslim populations, or even those that have Muslim majorities, extremist Islamists constitute a small minority. Yet across nations, the Islamists have achieved a good deal of ideological cohesion, and their violent methods have given them a prominence their small numbers would not otherwise warrant. In addition, it must be pointed out that among moderate Muslim populations, there is often some sympathy or even support for the Islamists. This does not necessarily mean that people want to see the Islamists' radical agendas enacted. But in some places (for example, Uzbekistan) Islamists are seen as the only effective opposition to a repressive government. In other places (such as southern Thailand, Mindanao, and Xinjiang) Islamist groups may be capitalizing on essentially nationalist aspirations. And throughout much of Muslim Asia, resentment of the West—especially the United States—is widespread. Thus a terrorist attack against, say, the Australian embassy in Jakarta might be applauded as punishment for Australia's participation in the U.S.-led war in Iraq, which some Muslims view as a war against fellow Muslims.

A multi-pronged approach may be the only way many Asian governments can hope to successfully confront the threat of Islamic terrorism. In many countries a determined military and law enforcement effort is needed to scatter Muslim insurgents in the field; destroy or dismantle the remote bases, training camps, and other infrastructure the Islamist terrorist organizations use; and uncover and break up terror cells, ideally before they have launched an attack. But it is equally important that governments deprive Islamist extremists of support among the general population. At a minimum, this requires that government measures designed to combat Islamist extremists do not also alienate moderate Muslims; in certain countries, some analysts believe, only fundamental reforms will guarantee long-term success against the Islamists.

The U.S. Interest and Role

For the United States, the stakes in Asia are extremely high. As a rule, Islamist terrorists seek the complete economic, cultural, and political withdrawal of the United States from Muslim lands—which obviously runs counter to U.S. strategic and commercial interests and is not a course of action American policymakers are prepared to entertain. But the goals of Islamist extremists extend beyond compelling the United States to withdraw from the Muslim world—at least, if one is to take at face value the rhetoric of such figures as Osama bin Laden. In his "Letter to America," released in November 2002, bin Laden spelled out his and his fellow

Islamists' vision for reforming American policy and society. First, he called on Americans to practice Islam and to discard "all the opinions, orders, theories and religions which contradict with the religion He sent down to His Prophet Muhammad (peace be upon him)." Second, he called upon America to "stop your oppression, lies, immorality and debauchery" and to reject "the immoral acts of fornication, homosexuality, intoxicants, gambling, and trading with interest. . . . It is saddening to tell you that you are the worst civilization witnessed by the history of mankind." On one level, the "Letter to America" may be seen principally as an attempt by bin Laden to justify the large-scale killing of American civilians. On another level, however, it may reflect the Islamists' profound misunderstanding of the nature of American society (which may be matched by the average American's misunderstanding of Islam and Islamism). In the final analysis, though, bin Laden's view precludes compromise or common ground with the United States.

The U.S. response to Islamist terrorism has featured a strong military component. Most prominent, of course, is the 2001 invasion of Afghanistan and the ouster of the Taliban. (Whether the 2003 Iraq war had any connection with the threat of Islamist terrorism is a matter of dispute between Bush administration critics and supporters.) Less obvious to the general public is the U.S. military presence in other countries of Asia. Since the attacks of September 11, 2001, the United States has been granted the right to operate military bases in the Central Asian nations of Uzbekistan, Kyrgyzstan, Tajikistan, and Kazakhstan. Such bases support operations in the ongoing fight against al-Qaeda and Taliban remnants, but they may also prove useful in combating other Islamist terrorist groups in Central Asia. The United States has also provided military aid and technical assistance to buttress Central Asian governments against Islamist threats. A U.S. troop presence exists in many other countries of Asia as well.

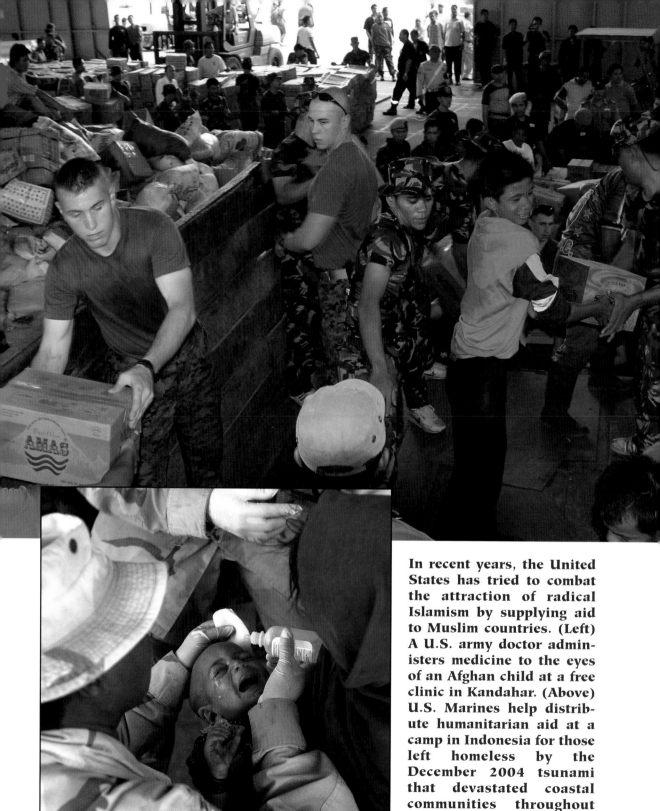

In recent years, the United States has tried to combat the attraction of radical Islamism by supplying aid to Muslim countries. (Left) A U.S. army doctor administers medicine to the eyes of an Afghan child at a free clinic in Kandahar. (Above) U.S. Marines help distribute humanitarian aid at a camp in Indonesia for those left homeless by the December 2004 tsunami that devastated coastal communities throughout the Indian Ocean region.

But the military component is only part of the equation. If Asian governments may ultimately need to "win hearts and minds" to forestall the rise of Islamist extremism, so too may the United States. For that reason, the U.S. government is engaged in a massive education and health campaign in Afghanistan, and to a certain extent, in Bangladesh and Indonesia as well; the U.S. government has also pressured Pakistan to reform its educational system. The focus of the educational efforts is on improving the madrassas or replacing them with schools that offer more balanced curricula and are supervised by the government. As of August 2004, the U.S. Congress had agreed to appropriate a total of about $5 billion for this purpose.

*   *   *   *   *

Almost nobody expects the fight against Islamist terrorism to be won overnight. To succeed, the countries of Asia, along with the United States, must be prepared to wage a long campaign—and any lapses in resolve could well have dire consequences.

1989	Soviet troops leave Afghanistan after losing a 10-year battle to control the country; Saudi millionaire Osama bin Laden brings together Arab mujahideen in the country to create al-Qaeda.
1991	The Soviet republics of Central Asia—all countries with Muslim populations—become independent with the dissolution of the Soviet Union.
1992	Bin Laden settles in Sudan, and al-Qaeda begins to form links with other Islamist groups in the region.
1993	In October a bomb explodes under the World Trade Center in New York City, killing 7 people and injuring more than 1,000 others; Ramzi Yousef, believed by many to have received funding from bin Laden, is eventually among those convicted in the bombing.
1994	Saudi Arabia strips bin Laden of citizenship.
1996	Bin Laden is asked to leave Sudan and returns to Afghanistan, where the Taliban militia is preparing to take over the government; he calls for a jihad against the United States. In a June attack blamed on al-Qaeda, 19 U.S. servicemen are killed by an explosion in the Khobar Towers military complex in Saudi Arabia.
1998	Ayman al-Zawahiri, the leader of Egyptian Islamic Jihad and bin Laden's personal physician, merges his group with al-Qaeda to form the World Islamic Front for Jihad against the Jews and Crusaders and becomes al-Qaeda's second-in-command; al-Qaeda is implicated in the car bombings of the U.S. embassies in Dar es Salaam, Tanzania, and Nairobi, Kenya, which kill 231 people, including 12 Americans.
2000	In October, in the port of Aden, Yemen, suicide bombers organized by al-Qaeda ram the side of the destroyer USS Cole with an explosives-laden boat, killing 17 American sailors. A series of explosions in the Philippine capital of Manila kills 22 people; Philippine and U.S. investigators link the attack to Jemaah Islamiyah (JI).

Chronology

2001   On September 11, teams of al-Qaeda–sponsored terror-ists hijack four commercial airliners, flying two into the World Trade Center in New York City and one into the Pentagon in Washington, D.C. (the fourth plane, en route to Washington, crashes in a field in western Pennsylvania); in all, nearly 3,000 people are killed in the attacks. The following day, U.S. president George W. Bush declares a "war on terrorism."

2002   In October the Philippine Islamist terror group Abu Sayyaf bombs a market in the city of Zamboanga del Sur, killing a U.S. solider and three other people; four more bomb attacks are blamed on Abu Sayyaf. In November bin Laden releases his "Letter to America," explaining his goals regarding the United States. In December JI carries out a bomb attack on two Bali nightclubs, killing more than 200 people and injuring dozens.

2003   A JI-planned attack on the Marriott Hotel in Jakarta, Indonesia, in August kills 12 and injures 150.

al-Qaeda—an international Islamist terror organization established in Afghanistan in 1989; led by Osama bin Laden, it orchestrated the attacks of September 11, 2001, as well as many others against U.S. and other targets.

animist—characterized by the belief in spirits in nature and inanimate objects.

burka—a dark head-to-toe dress worn by women in accordance with Islamic code; it is used in Afghanistan, Saudi Arabia, and parts of Pakistan.

caliphate—an Islamic state ruled by a caliph (a Muslim spiritual and temporal leader).

imam—a mosque prayer leader, often the community religious leader and judge.

jihad—a holy war waged on behalf of Islam; some Muslims interpret this as a call to arms, while others see it as a personal struggle to maintain spiritual discipline.

madrassa—an Islamic educational establishment in which students focus solely on studying the Qur'an and learning Arabic and the teachings of the early Islamic leaders.

mosque—a Muslim house of worship.

mujahideen—Islamic holy warriors, or warriors involved in a holy war (jihad).

Qur'an—Islam's holy scriptures.

Salafism—a fundamentalist Islamic ideology holding that only the teachings and practices of Muhammad, his companions, and his four immediate successors as caliph are valid; it advocates a return to the Islam of these righteous forefathers.

secular—non-religious.

Sharia—Islamic law.

Shia—the second-largest branch of Islam, which claims about 15 percent of the religion's followers worldwide and which rejects the legitimacy of all Muslim caliphs not directly descended from the prophet Muhammad through the line of Ali.

Glossary

Sunni—Islam's dominant branch, with about 80 percent of the believers worldwide; Sunnis recognize no single human authority in religious matters.

syncretic—characterized by the blending of different religions, practices, or philosophies.

Taliban—a Salafist organization, originally formed by Afghan refugees studying in Pakistan's Islamic schools, which ruled Afghanistan from 1996 to 2001.

theocracy—a government whose officials claim to be divinely guided.

Turkic—any of a group of Asian peoples speaking a language related to modern Turkish (including Turkish, Azeri, Turkmen, Uzbek, Kazakh, Kyrgyz, and Uygur).

Wahhabi—a member of an extremely conservative Salafist sect, which is named after the 18th-century reformer Muhammad ibn Abd al-Wahhab and which is the official form of Islam in Saudi Arabia (though Saudis tend to avoid using the term to describe themselves because they consider it misleading).

umma—the worldwide community of Muslims.

zakat—the Muslim religious obligation to contribute a percentage of one's income to charity.

Editor's note: Because Arab speakers and Islamic scholars transcribe names and terms in different ways, there is no general consensus over the transliteration of Arabic words into Latin script.

Abuza, Zachary. *Militant Islam in Southeast Asia: Crucible of Terror.* Boulder, Colo., and London: Lynne Rienner Publications, 2003.

Algar, Hamid. *Wahhabism: A Critical Essay.* Oneonta, N.Y.: Islamic Publications International, 2002.

Gunaratna, Rohan. *Inside Al Qaeda: Global Network of Terror.* London: Hurst & Co., 2002.

Kepel, Gilles. *Jihad: The Trail of Political Islam.* Cambridge, Mass.: Belknap Press of Harvard University Press, 2002.

Laqueur, Walter, editor. *Voices of Terror.* New York: Reed Press, 2004.

Santhanam, K., et al. *Jihadis in Jammu and Kashmir: A Portrait Gallery.* New Delhi, India: Sage Publications India, 2003.

Viorst, Milton. *In the Shadow of the Prophet: The Struggle for the Soul of Islam.* Boulder, Colo.: Westview Press, 2002.

Al-Zayyat, Montasser. *The Road to Al-Qaeda: The Story of bin Laden's Right-Hand Man.* London: Pluto Press, 2004.

Internet Resources

www.terrorismanswers.org

This site, maintained by the Council on Foreign Relations, tackles the most recent issues concerning terrorist groups in Asia and the rest of the world; it also profiles the individual groups and their beliefs.

www.crisisweb.org/home/index.cfm

The International Crisis Group monitors developments in countries that are embroiled in conflict. Read about the political circumstances under which many Asian Islamists live and operate.

http://www.ict.org.il/

The home page of the International Policy Institute for Counter-Terrorism offers articles, news, and analysis of the worldwide fight against terrorism.

http://www.csmonitor.com/specials/terrorism/start.html?leftNav Include

This excellent interactive guide, managed by the *Christian Science Monitor*, investigates terrorists throughout history and their various struggles.

http://usinfo.state.gov/is/international_security/terrorism/ terror_global.html

This online guide, "Terrorism at a Glance," presents a working definition of terrorism as well as the official U.S. stance against it. It also briefly summarizes the government's strategy for fighting the war on terror.

Numbers in **bold italic** refer to captions.

Index

Index

Picture Credits

The **FOREIGN POLICY RESEARCH INSTITUTE (FPRI)** served as editorial consultants for the GROWTH AND INFLUENCE OF ISLAM IN THE NATIONS OF ASIA AND CENTRAL ASIA series. FPRI is one of the nation's oldest "think tanks." The Institute's Middle East Program focuses on Gulf security, monitors the Arab-Israeli peace process, and sponsors an annual conference for teachers on the Middle East, plus periodic briefings on key developments in the region.

Among the FPRI's trustees is a former Secretary of State and a former Secretary of the Navy (and among the FPRI's former trustees and interns, two current Undersecretaries of Defense), not to mention two university presidents emeritus, a foundation president, and several active or retired corporate CEOs.

The scholars of FPRI include a former aide to three U.S. Secretaries of State, a Pulitzer Prize–winning historian, a former president of Swarthmore College and a Bancroft Prize–winning historian, and two former staff members of the National Security Council. And the FPRI counts among its extended network of scholars—especially its Inter-University Study Groups—representatives of diverse disciplines, including political science, history, economics, law, management, religion, sociology, and psychology.

DR. HARVEY SICHERMAN is president and director of the Foreign Policy Research Institute in Philadelphia, Pennsylvania. He has extensive experience in writing, research, and analysis of U.S. foreign and national security policy, both in government and out. He served as Special Assistant to Secretary of State Alexander M. Haig Jr. and as a member of the Policy Planning Staff of Secretary of State James A. Baker III. Dr. Sicherman was also a consultant to Secretary of the Navy John F. Lehman Jr. (1982–1987) and Secretary of State George Shultz (1988).

A graduate of the University of Scranton (B.S., History, 1966), Dr. Sicherman earned his Ph.D. at the University of Pennsylvania (Political Science, 1971), where he received a Salvatori Fellowship. He is author or editor of numerous books and articles, including *America the Vulnerable: Our Military Problems and How to Fix Them* (FPRI, 2002) and *Palestinian Autonomy, Self-Government and Peace* (Westview Press, 1993). He edits *Peacefacts*, an FPRI bulletin that monitors the Arab-Israeli peace process.

DR. MICHAEL RADU is senior fellow and co-chairman of the Center on Terrorism, Counterterrorism and Homeland Security at the Foreign Policy Research Institute in Philadelphia, Pennsylvania. He has published or edited 11 books, mostly on political violence and terrorism, and hundreds of scholarly and popular articles on those topics.